Difficult People at Work

How to deal with:
- credit grabbers
- tyrants
- space cadets
- saboteurs

... and 20 other challenging personality types

BusinessManagement
DAILY

EDITOR
Kathy Shipp

EDITORIAL DIRECTOR
Patrick DiDomenico

ASSOCIATE PUBLISHER
Adam Goldstein

PUBLISHER
Phillip A. Ash

ISBN 1-880024-10-1

"This publication is designed to provide accurate and authoritative information in regard to the subject matter covered. It is sold with the understanding that the publisher is not engaged in rendering legal, accounting or other professional service. If legal advice or other expert assistance is required, the services of a competent professional person should be sought."—*From a Declaration of Principles jointly adopted by a committee of the American Bar Association and a committee of publishers and associations.*

Contents

Introduction

Working with difficult people can be, well—difficult. Staff productivity suffers because Subordinate A is an underachiever and Subordinate B is a bit of a bully. Colleague X keeps putting you down at meetings, and Colleague Y grabs credit for your best ideas. To top it all off, your boss is a control freak who drives you nuts. At times you're tempted to quit: Who needs all these difficult people! But upon reflection, you stay because you know you can count on encountering "challenging" personalities wherever you go.

Knowing how to work with difficult people is not a skill that comes naturally. However, if there's no escape from difficult people, there *is* a way to lessen the pain. If you're willing to make the effort, you can master the skills that will help you cope with troublesome personalities.

This Report is your guide to identifying and dealing with the 24 difficult personalities you're most likely to encounter in the workplace—whether as bosses, subordinates or peers. It tells you what makes each one of them tick and then offers you specific guidelines for dealing with each one. You'll learn:

- ***The art of productive confrontation.*** Most executives don't know how to confront people effectively. They either blow up, don't say anything (and eat themselves up inside) or act out their anger in manipulative ways. This Report will teach you how to deal with difficult people at work.
- ***How to make an obstructive employee productive.*** Today, it is difficult to fire subordinates unless they're dishonest or blatantly out of line. In many companies, it can take years of document gathering before you can get rid of someone. Instead, learn how to make the difficult person a productive team member.
- ***How to resist intimidation.*** The biggest problem managers have is that they're too easily intimidated. This Report will teach you the delicate art of resisting intimidation without antagonizing would-be intimidators. You'll learn that you have a lot more power than you realize, even as a subordinate.
- ***How to meet the needs of your staff.*** Effective management comes from working with people and meeting their needs, not through confrontation. Too often, managers wind up doing too much of the work themselves because they can't manage difficult people. Then they're so busy that they don't have the time to manage anyone. This Report will teach you how to analyze and work with difficult people in ways that benefit you both.

How to find what you need

To make it easy to find what you need, this Report is divided into four main sections. Each section corresponds to one of the four basic types of difficult personalities—power players, indirect aggressors (who block you without directly confronting you), underachievers and others. In each section, we take a look at the root personality traits of each type first, and then we examine the various difficult personalities who share these root traits. We tell you how each type operates and offer you strategies for dealing with that personality. Even the most difficult interpersonal encounters involve at least two people, so we end the Report with a short section focused on *you*.

Once you make the effort, you'll begin to notice what makes people tick. You'll get flashes of insight into why people act differently depending on the situation and the people involved. Your people skills will snowball.

Personal growth is important in all of life's stages. You need to keep growing to deal effectively with others. When you start putting into practice the suggestions you'll find in this Report, you'll jump-start the growth process. At first, you may feel uneasy and uncomfortable because you'll be interacting with people differently. But that discomfort will disappear in time, and the benefits of your changed behavior will become a permanent asset.

Look at all the applicable categories when you're deciding the best way to deal with a difficult person. Very rarely does anyone fit neatly into one personality category; human nature is infinitely varied. Follow the recommendations for the category that best fits the person. For example, you may be dealing with a mercurial tyrant. Mercurials are fairly benign, but tyrants are the most dangerous kind of difficult personality. In this case, you would follow the recommendations for dealing with a tyrant, and use the mercurial description and suggestions to give yourself further insight.

Reading this Report won't change the personalities you're dealing with. If you follow the guidelines, however, it will change your relationships for the better. You'll increase productivity, reduce stress and be more in control than you ever dreamed possible. You and your colleagues will feel better, and you'll all be more productive.

Power Players

Power players have to abuse, manipulate or control somebody: That's how they feel good about themselves. Somewhere in the past, they were probably abused, manipulated or controlled, and they can deal with people only if they are in the one-up position.

We are not excusing power players' behavior because they had unhappy childhoods, but it helps to know that these ogres were made, not born.

Power players tend to see the world in black and white. They're either on top of the heap or at the bottom. For them, there's no such thing as moderate success or reasonable ambition. They tend to be grandiose, bucking for CEO or nothing—even if they have to climb over a pile of innocent subordinates and colleagues to get there.

Most recognizable power players are bosses because, as bosses, they're in a position to wield power obviously and effectively. But there are power players at all levels and in all positions; even the mail sorter can be a power player if he's steaming open the mail to get the goods on someone. In fact, subordinate power players can be the most insidious. Before you know it, they've maneuvered themselves into your job.

Not all power players are bad guys, however. They range all the way from the dreadfully insecure to the downright evil.

Many power players are quivering jellyfish inside. There's a direct correlation between needing to have power over others and feeling powerless inside. This is why many power players act terribly hurt when they're outfoxed or outgunned. Inside, they feel weak and vulnerable. Even when their behavior has been nakedly aggressive, they simply don't understand what they did to deserve an "attack."

Neurotics vs. narcissistic power players

Psychologically, there are two basic power-player types: neurotics and narcissists. To come up with effective self-defense tactics, it's helpful to know which one you're dealing with.

Neurotic: The neurotic power player is driven by insecurity. He was brought up by perfectionist parents who told him he was never good enough. He's the kid who comes home with a B+ and gets a hard time from Mom and Dad because it isn't an A. He's constantly trying to prove his worth by accruing more power.

What he doesn't realize is that his need for power is addictive. He'll never have enough to relax and feel good about himself.

The neurotic power player has to control everything and everyone around him. He can't let go for a minute. However, he's not as difficult to deal with as the narcissistic power player because he is capable of feeling bad about his excesses. If you can locate and push his guilt button, he'll back off. It may also help if you can find out something about the power player's past; it may give you some leverage in dealing with him.

Narcissistic: This type of power player is really dangerous. He has no conscience or guilt; he's capable of just about anything. He was brought up by parents who either totally ignored him or treated him like a little prince no matter what mayhem he caused. Like the mythical Narcissus, who gazed into the water at the perfection of his own image until he died, the narcissistic power player is totally consumed with himself. Only *his* needs are important; yours don't even exist.

Observation: It pays to keep the myth of Narcissus in mind when dealing with a narcissist. Try to get him to become so enamored of himself that he loses touch with reality and wastes away.

The power player's self-image

For power players, being one-up isn't a matter of preference—it's a matter of life and death. A loss of power is the same as a loss of self. If they're not powerful, they don't know who they are, and this is extremely frightening. The loss of identity is a kind of death. Power players will fight bitterly to keep their power and to avoid losing that vital sense of self.

Many power players are so focused on their image that they can't let it slip for a moment. They always have to appear to be in charge—unmoved by things that would move others. They must be the center of attention. This is why direct confrontation is almost never effective with a power player. He'll be so threatened that he'll immediately go on the defensive.

Dealing with power players

The best way to deal with a power player is by playing to his or her need for power. Give him what he wants, and you'll have him eating out of your hand. To get what *you* want from the power player, you've got to make it crystal clear that meeting your needs will make him more, not less, powerful.

You'll find specific recommendations for dealing with each type of power player in the rest of this section.

Tyrants

Most of us are used to thinking of tyrants as fearsome foreign dictators. But psychologists and business consultants Mardy Grothe and Peter Wylie point out in their book *Problem Bosses* (Ballantine) that "organizations in America are not bastions of freedom and democracy. As a matter of fact, when we look at the presidents of most organizations, they remind us of dukes and princes and counts who rule over their fiefdoms with almost supreme power.... The rights we take for granted as citizens, like the rights of free speech and assembly, in many ways stop when you walk through your company's front door."

Many corporations are benevolent dictatorships, with a president and top management who treat employees fairly. Others, like some of the newer team-oriented companies, are striving for democracy. But some corporations are run by tyrants. If a tyrant is at the head of your company and you don't like him, quitting may be your only recourse. But if the tyrant is your boss, and top management is rational, there may be some hope.

How tyrants operate

To those of us who govern our lives in an ethical, moral way and consider the needs of others, it may seem a cosmic injustice that tyrants are so successful. In a just world, they wouldn't be. But their lack of ethics and morality is the reason they get what they want so often. They're ruthless and implacable; they will do anything to succeed, and they don't have the scruples that inhibit the rest of us. These traits allow them to do things that most people would find unthinkable.

Tyrants use fear, coercion and terrorism to control others. The true forms of command, participation and education are foreign concepts to tyrants. According to psychologist Bill Knaus, "Tyrants put on good fronts, but they actually get an emotional high from causing harm."

Tyrants all operate under subjective value systems, and their actions are arbitrary. *Example:* The tyrannical boss who cancels your vacation because he decides it's too busy to let you go, even though the workload hasn't changed at all.

Tyrants hire people they consider to be weak, people they think they can bend to their will. Tyrants punish those who are foolish enough to ask questions and threaten their power. They consciously work to make others feel inferior. Some tactics tyrants use include:

- Using lies and distortions to achieve their ends.
- Disregarding ideas and suggestions from out-of-favor people.
- Ignoring unfavorable facts.
- Blaming others for their own mistakes.
- Using glowing rhetoric and cosmetic changes to create a bright, but false, picture.
- Using character generalizations, such as describing out-of-favor people as busybodies, malcontents or traitors.
- Controlling the flow of information: The tyrant sees facts and ideas as dangerous unless they support his position.

Over time, tyrants get worse, not better. Their destructive impulses escalate until, at the pinnacle of their arrogance, their systems crumble around them. At this point, it often becomes obvious to others that they've gone too far and caused too much harm. *Example:* Frank Lorenzo. In trying to destroy the pilots' union, he destroyed Eastern Airlines. That's why the pilots were so intent on getting another buyer for Eastern. They felt they couldn't negotiate with the tyrannical Lorenzo.

Understanding tyrants

Tyrants are narcissistic power players because they have no empathy. They actually enjoy abusing people, and they have no interest in changing their behavior. Unlike bullies, who act out of inner insecurity, tyrants and malignants are missing vital parts of human nature—a conscience, empathy, morals and ethics.

In her book *For Your Own Good* (Farrar Straus), German psychoanalyst Alice Miller explores hidden cruelty in child-rearing as being the root of violence and tyranny. Chances are, your boss was humiliated or hurt in some way as a child; he is compensating for that hurt by being sadistic to his employees.

Tyrants are resentment-anger types, says psychologist and personnel specialist H.D. Johns, author of *From Fear to Fury* (Vantage Press). They're angry people whose anger is fueled by resentment. When something goes wrong, they project their anger outward and blame it on someone else. Their life stance is "I'm OK, but you're not OK." They believe in doing unto others before they do unto you.

They were often brought up very strictly and weren't allowed to feel any emotion as children, Johns explains. So their anger goes underground, eventually surfacing as resentment. What they resent, they want to destroy. Thus, tyrannical managers resent competent employees who threaten to show them up.

In a frightening way, resentment-anger types set about getting rid of people and situations that threaten them in their daily lives. They're obsessed with winning and terrified of losing. As adults, they become powerful and dangerous leaders. They often move up quickly in highly structured societies and organizations because they act expediently at all times; for them, the end *always* justifies the means. The good news, according to Johns, is that resentment-anger types are fairly rare. They're only about 1 percent of the population.

Strategies to unseat a tyrant

Tyrants are the most trying of all the difficult types to deal with because they're unmoved by normal human feelings, such as the desire to be liked by others. The only thing they understand is power—and that power has to be massive to be effective.

The best way to deal with tyrants is not to deal with them. Avoid them when you see them coming. If a tyrant is CEO and the board belongs to him, you might as well look for another job. But if there's a rational, objective management above him that has the good of the company at heart, a tyrant can be unseated. In fact, tyrants often bring themselves down, as Frank Lorenzo did, because they go too far. This makes them vulnerable.

To unseat a tyrant, Dr. Knaus recommends being far better organized than he is at pulling together a coalition. You have to expose the tyrant in a pretty dramatic way to put him in a position where he has to run for his life.

Caution: Tyrants can be extremely dangerous when cornered. Be prepared to lose. If the tyrant has the power to do so, he'll impose a crushing defeat—he'll try to ruin your reputation as well as fire you.

To prevail against a tyrant, you need:
- The facts on your side.
- An objective top executive who is senior to the tyrant.
- Willingness to seize the moment. This means taking risks when the time is ripe to make the right assertion against the tyrant. We've all kicked ourselves for missing such moments.
- Guts enough to stand up to the tyrant's rage.
- Willingness to lose.
- Ability to get key allies, people who are important and influential, on your side.

Here are some strategies you might use. Look into the politics of the situation. Discover who has the most to gain by unseating the tyrant, and approach that person. Keep in mind that the tyrant's subordinates may have an interest in keeping him there. Dr. Knaus notes, "I've unseated a few tyrants in my day, but it involves an enormous effort, a lot of organization, allies in key positions, facts and data. It's hard to knock off very high-level people because they usually surround themselves with board members of their own choosing… But at lower levels, if you can show that the person is a detriment to the organization, you have a chance.

"Usually, unseating a tyrant involves timing and pacing. You have to time your move to occur when he's at the pinnacle of arrogance because he's most vulnerable when he thinks he's strongest. You have to approach people in the organization who are unhappy and who are willing to leak information. You have to be careful about whom you trust, but you can't be paranoid. It's entirely possible and feasible to move tyrants out because they're often more interested in political gains than productive pursuits. You can almost always cause them a lot of heartburn by producing solid results."

The best time to unseat a tyrant is during a time of crisis. In times of crisis, tyrants usually can't rise to the occasion. They'll look for stronger people to take over; then they'll get rid of them when the crisis has passed. If you're one of these people, make your contribution clear to top management.

If you can't unseat a tyrant, you have various options. Under some circumstances, tyrants can be dealt with—at least for finite lengths of time. Working for a tyrant indefinitely can be quite destructive to your sense of self, but you can learn to cope with one until you get a better job or transfer out of his department.

Muriel Solomon, author of *Working With Difficult People* (Prentice Hall), says your goal should be to get the tyrant to treat you in a civil, courteous manner and to stop being so overbearing. She recommends these tactics:
- ***Prepare to act.*** Stop accepting the situation. If you do nothing, the wounds he inflicts on you will fester until you finally blow up or break down.
- ***Appear firm, strong and unemotional.*** If you reveal that you're weak and angry, the tyrant will try harder to dominate you. Let him rage. You must appear serene and not a threat to his majesty's self-image.
- ***Use tact to get his attention and respect.*** Telling him he's wrong will make him seek revenge. Instead, ask questions that show you want to talk.

Demonstrate *understanding* for his point of view, and then insert your own perspective.

- **Try strategic yielding.** Dr. Gerald Piaget, author of *Control Freaks* (Bantam, Doubleday, Dell), recommends this tactic, but he acknowledges that it's very difficult to pull off. There may be times when resistance isn't working, or it isn't worth the cost. Go along with the tyrant in these cases. Admit to him that he might be right. Emphasize the areas where you agree. Consciously choose to give in—because it is in your best interest, *for the time being.*

Bullies

Bullies get their way through pushiness or outright intimidation. The bully is often an entrepreneur or a self-made person. Having started his own business or pulled himself up by his bootstraps, he's convinced that he always knows what's best.

The bully needs to be in control. He sees himself as a "take-charge" guy who can't delegate responsibility because he might lose everything he's gained. According to psychologist Piaget, bullies are found among managers and executives who climbed the career ladder by setting goals and using everything within their power to reach those goals. Over the years, they got into the habit of controlling people and things to get what they wanted. They've become almost superstitious about operating in any other way. "One slip-up and I could lose everything I've gained," they think.

The bully's need for control can make him incredibly overbearing. He can publicly humiliate you, use guilt to manipulate you to do his bidding or blow up and make scenes to intimidate you. He may threaten to fire you and generally treat you like an unruly 2-year-old instead of a respected adult.

The bully is, above all, overwhelming. His entire demeanor expresses "aggression." According to psychologist Robert Bramson, in his book *Coping With Difficult People* (Doubleday), bullies are "arbitrary and often arrogant in tone. When criticizing something you've said or done, they seem to attack not just the particular behavior, but *you,* and they do so in an accusatory way. They are contemptuous of their victims, considering them to be inferior people who deserve to be bullied and disparaged."

Dr. Bramson thinks bullies are frequently able to gain authority because they "possess tremendous power in interpersonal situations. Such power comes largely from the typical responses their behavior arouses: con-

fusion, mental or physical flight or a sense of helpless frustration that leads to tears or a tantrum-like rage." But pushing people around goes only so far for the bully. At some point, subordinates will start to resist.

Bullies, unlike tyrants, are not narcissists; they are neurotics. This means that their sense of entitlement is a defense against their inner feelings of insecurity and unworthiness, rather than an intrinsic personality flaw.

According to Dr. Piaget, bullies are "apt to be perfectionists or people who have overcome adversity, disabilities or discrimination."

Like the schoolyard bully, he is compensating for what he's ashamed of—such as being poor, not being able to read or being abused at home. He may have been taunted as a child because he was overweight, stuttered or had a learning disability. Whatever the reason, all the thunder and lightning he throws at others camouflages what's underneath.

The bully is terrified that someone will discover his hidden vulnerabilities, so he remains aloof from everyone—both at the office and in his personal life. He can't let down his guard and show any weakness or softness. If he did let down his guard and show his vulnerable side, of course, his staff would like him more and cooperate with him. He might even turn into an effective manager instead of someone whom employees automatically resent and resist.

Incredulous as it seems, the aggressive boss who claims always to be right, never wavers for an instant and projects total self-assurance is really a fragile little child inside. The amount of his bullying directly correlates to the amount of inner insecurity he feels. If a bully starts feeling better about himself, his bullying behavior will decrease.

Observation: If you can visualize the frightened child the bully is frantically trying to hide, it may help you control your anger and make him easier to deal with.

Dealing with a bully boss

The traditional wisdom about a schoolyard bully holds true for a corporate bully as well: You have to stand up to him. Bullies can smell weakness in their adversaries, and they will move in for the kill. They may hate themselves in the morning, but the smell of blood is irresistible. Like a schoolyard bully, however, they will often back down when you show them you're willing to fight.

- **Send the right signal physically.** When you're attacked, your body language will indicate whether you're intimidated. If your shoulders droop and your eyes drop, the bully will get the message that you are intimidated and really lay it on. To send the opposite message, take a deep breath, which draws your frame up, look the bully square in the eye and remain still.

- *Let the bully talk;* don't interrupt. If you ask anything, ask open-ended questions beginning with "who," "what," "when," "where" and "how." Ask permission to take notes so that you can get this matter resolved. After you ask a question, be quiet, and let the bully talk as you take notes. This will make him think he's getting results, which will calm him down and may make him stop seeing you as an enemy.

- *Don't expect to feel comfortable.* When standing up to a bully, you will feel confused, overwhelmed, angry, hurt and afraid. That's what the bully is counting on: He uses those feelings to intimidate people. Even if you feel distraught and can't say just the right thing, do say something, anything, to counter his onslaught. Don't be overwhelmed by your fear and cave in.

- *If the bully has lost his temper,* Dr. Bramson recommends giving him time to run down. "If the person you are confronting is yelling at you, crying angrily or reacting in a noisy, emotional manner, stand pat for a while to give him time to run down. Remain in place, look directly at him and wait. When the attack loses momentum, jump into the situation."

- *Don't compete with a bully.* Psychiatrist John M. Oldham, co-author of *Personality Self-Portrait, Why You Think, Work, Love and Act the Way You Do* (Bantam), says you should "never try to undermine this person's authority or unseat him or her… If you do find yourself competing with a bully, allow him or her to save face in case you win. Otherwise, you'll find yourself with a very powerful enemy."

- *Appeal to reason, not to feelings.* Aggressive people, says Dr. Oldham, give very little weight to how a person feels; showing emotion won't help you much. Use reason to make your point. Illustrate how your plan or approach benefits the aggressive person.

- *Use your knowledge of the bully's inner insecurity.* His rage is coming from some inner fear. Analyze what that fear is, and address the fear instead of the rage. Talk to the bully about it in a nonaccusatory way. *Example:* Len, Janet's boss, saw Janet talking on the phone for an extended length of time. He assumed it was a personal call, when actually she was talking to a client. Instead of waiting until she got off the phone, he stood over her desk and yelled, "I know you're on a personal call. Why don't you do some work for a change?" The client heard this, and Janet was terribly humiliated.

Instead of yelling back that it wasn't a personal call, she finished talking to the client and then went into Len's office to ask to speak to him. She had figured out that Len's fear was that he'd be taken advantage of and played for a fool. He had an almost paranoid fear that his employees were taking long lunches, making personal calls and taking supplies home.

Janet said, "Len, I know you're worried about people taking advantage of you, but I would never do that. You know I'm a good worker who does more than is expected of me." Len had to agree that this was true. Janet continued, "I felt very humiliated by your yelling at me so loudly that our client could hear. We may have lost a sale. Next time you have a problem with me, please call me into your office and let's discuss it privately." After Janet said this, Len actually apologized and promised to do what she asked.

Why this strategy worked:

- Janet addressed Len's fear instead of blaming him.
- She implicated him in his own bad behavior by saying "our" client, and "we" may have lost a sale.
- Instead of telling him what was wrong with him, she used an "I" statement, expressing how his behavior affected her.
- She came up with a solution he could live with— calling her into his office instead of making a scene.

You can talk to some bullies. Many are simply overreactors. An overreactor tends to lose her cool fairly quickly. The slightest provocation results in anger or hysteria. The bully herself may think this is a problem and feel guilty about losing her temper.

If your boss is that kind of bully, Dr. Grothe thinks she may be a good candidate for either a one-on-one or a low-key group discussion about the situation. Dr. Grothe recommends talking frankly from the heart about the impact her behavior has on you. Try to get her to modify the offending behavior.

Observation: Employees often need to ask themselves what motive the boss has to change. Even if you've got an overreactor bully boss who wants to change after you confront him or her, the chances of that happening increase dramatically if you can also ask your boss the question, "What can I do for you?"

Whenever you can sit down with a boss or an employee and mediate a performance agreement, the chance that both of you will make lasting behavior changes is increased.

Handling the staff bully

We all know how hard it is to deal with a bully boss. It can also be difficult to confront a bullying subordinate because bullies are always intimidating. But if it comes to your attention that one of your managers is bullying his staff, you need to confront him assertively and point out his bullying tactics.

Bullies are often unaware of their behavior. Some feedback from above will enable many of them to modify their own behavior.

- *Give specific examples.* Tell the person how *you* would have handled specific situations that you feel he has mishandled.
- *Provide education about good management.* Explain that positive encouragement motivates better than bullying—every time. Send the person to a workshop or seminar on management skills, or give him a self-help book on how to handle employees effectively.
- *Monitor his performance.* Don't undermine his authority with his employees, but do talk to his staffers about whether or not he's controlling his temper.

Credit Grabbers

Credit grabbers can be peers, bosses and occasionally even subordinates. But bosses are the most difficult credit grabbers to deal with. In fact, credit grabbing is one of the most common complaints Dr. Grothe hears about bosses. "Employees bust their butts, work real hard, but when the boss goes to those upper-level executive committee meetings, he talks about the accomplishments of the department as if he or she is responsible for all the success," Dr. Grothe says.

In some ways the boss *is* partially responsible for the success of his staffers. When he manages a team effectively and that team does well, the boss deserves credit.

Example: Lee Iacocca. There were thousands of employees who fought hard to bring Chrysler back to life. As far as the press was concerned, however, it was Lee Iacocca who accomplished this goal. He was the manager who motivated an entire company. But if you talked to the executive vice presidents and upper-level managers at Chrysler, they'd probably say, "Hey, what about our contribution? Lee is getting all the credit, but we worked hard too."

So this is not a clear-cut issue. The boss will deny he's taking credit for his employees' work, but he will insist on taking credit for being a good manager. The many employees who aren't singled out or mentioned will feel overlooked and resentful as a result.

Dealing with inadvertent credit grabbers

Some bosses take credit almost unconsciously. They need to be educated about what's appropriate and what employees' needs are.

- *Sit down with your boss and talk to him* as an individual or as a member of the group. *Good statement:* "Look, when you present the accomplishments of the organization as something that you're primarily responsible for, I feel left out. I've worked hard too. I'd like more credit for my accomplishments, not just personally, but when you're talking to the upper echelons in our company or in other organizations."
- *Cite the kinds of bosses who do give credit.* Dr. Grothe suggests using retired Gen. Norman Schwartzkopf as a real-life example. When Schwartzkopf talked about victory, he tried to single out what this person and that person did. He has a humble quality that makes people want to work harder for him.

Psychologist Knaus calls the credit grabber who takes credit for everything a "mind pirate." This is the worst kind of credit grabber. According to Knaus, some mind-pirate bosses use tyrannical procedures as well. Initially, they may just ask for information and try to solicit your ideas without crediting you. If you withhold information, they try to find leverage points—your salary, your job security or a threat to send you to "Siberia."

A good example of a mind pirate was the boss in the movie *9 to 5*. The women in the office did all the work, but when their boss talked to his boss, he took all the credit.

In many organizations, the mind pirate is the top guy—a situation that puts the subordinates in a real bind. This was the problem Lee Iacocca ran into with Henry Ford. Iacocca talks about how threatened Henry Ford was when Iacocca started to get all the good publicity at Ford Motor Co. Iacocca tried to make it work at Ford, but his credit-grabbing boss was the most powerful person in the organization. Ford eventually fired Iacocca, which was the best thing that ever happened to him. If Ford hadn't fired him, Iacocca might have languished at Ford for another five or 10 years, unfulfilled and unhappy.

Although the mind pirate is most often a boss, he may also be a peer, a subordinate or someone you interact with casually. Whoever the person is, the mind pirate isn't going to become a nice guy, but you can modify his behavior in some cases. The following strategies can be useful:

- *Negotiate with a mind-pirate boss.* *Good statement:* "If my idea has merit, I'd like to join with you in some way to gain reasonable recognition for it. How might we accomplish that?" If you're dealing with someone remotely reasonable and you have a lot of good ideas, the person may decide to share the credit rather than kill the goose that's laying the golden eggs. *Example:* One manager wrote down the name of her boss on all her reports so he'd take credit—but not *all* the credit.

Caution: If you're dealing with an out-and-out narcissist who's very self-centered and distorts much of what he hears, he may think that he's the one who thought up your good idea. That makes it *his* idea. With this type, you have to be sure to document all your ideas.

- *Send a summary memorandum.* After meetings where the mind-pirate boss tries to pick your brain, send him a memo summarizing the ideas you contributed and suggesting alternate courses of action. Be polite. Tell him it was a pleasure to work with him on these projects. Stress your interest in contributing to the organization's overall progress.
- *Send a copy of the summary memo* outlining your suggestions to someone else in the organization who is likely to be supportive. This person should be informed of your ideas.
- *Publish your ideas in article form* to make them part of the public record. *Alternative:* Publicize and distribute your ideas in memorandum form.
- *Don't brainstorm with the mind pirate one-on-one if you can avoid it.* And be careful about sharing your ideas with those who curry favor by passing what they hear along to the credit grabbers.
- *If all else fails, quit.* Dr. Grothe says there are some bosses you just shouldn't work for, and the mind pirate is often one of them.

Observation: Sometimes you're lucky when one of these bosses fires you. Otherwise, you might have been stuck working for a bad boss for a long time. Life is too short to spend month after month, year after year working for parasitic bosses who will continue to damage your self-esteem, your career and, eventually, your health.

Malignants

Although you have to deal with tyrants and control freaks (see Section 4) as bosses, malignants will be either your subordinates or your peers. A malignant in a position of real power immediately becomes a tyrant.

You read about malignant people regularly in the newspapers. There's the handsome young man who cons an old lady into giving him her life savings. Or the pillar of the community who has a foolproof get-rich-quick investment scheme to funnel the money of lifelong friends into her own pocket.

Malignants are consummate narcissists. They understand only their own needs. They have no empathy, and they will stop at nothing to achieve their ends. They see you the way a hunter sees a deer; they will take whatever they want, any way they can. They will lie, steal, cheat and may even wind up resorting to violence if they are backed into a corner.

Malignant people are dangerous. Avoid them at all costs. The ordinary private citizen just doesn't have the emotional, financial or legal resources to deal with anyone this nasty.

Often, the problem is spotting them soon enough to get out of their way. Most malignants don't look evil. They're usually more attractive and charming than the rest of us. If they looked like thugs, it would be easy to steer clear of them. But they're more likely to look like the overly cooperative subordinate who claims only to want to help you. Mysterious things happen when he's around, however: Important papers disappear from your desk—people find out things about you they aren't supposed to know—or your boss looks at you strangely, and he asks about your health when you aren't sick.

Here's an example. Jack, a vice president in charge of sales at a paper supply company, hired Terence as a marketing assistant. Terence was a handsome, charming young man of about 30, who said he'd just gotten to town. He couldn't provide any references because he said he'd worked for another paper supply company that had gone out of business recently.

Jack happened to know someone else who had worked for that company, and he asked about Terence. His friend said Terence had the reputation of being a scheming, conniving, vicious creep. The reference was so bad that Jack didn't think it could possibly fit the bright, articulate, well-dressed, extremely polite young man he'd interviewed. Jack decided there must be some mistake, and he hired Terence anyway.

After a few months, Jack started to wonder if he had made a mistake. Terence came to work late, spent an enormous amount of time making personal calls and didn't seem to know much about the paper business. Once Jack overheard Terence talking on the phone about something that sounded like a big drug deal at a company warehouse, but he dismissed it as too far-fetched. Every time Jack confronted Terence about his lateness or poor performance, Terence would come up with a logical excuse. He was so convincing, Jack kept giving him another chance.

Finally, Terence failed to show up for a crucial meeting, and Jack called him into his office and fired him. With a twisted smile, Terence said Jack had better not do that because he'd falsified the computer records to show that Jack had been using company property to smuggle drugs.

Actually, Terence had been using the company's trucks and warehouses to smuggle large shipments of cocaine. He had set it up so that, if questions arose, it would look like Jack was the culprit. Jack was in shock. He didn't know what to do or where to turn.

It's hard to say how people get to be this malignant. Most of us are instilled with a sense of right and wrong at an early age, which provides us with a check on our behavior. We might be tempted to cheat, but our consciences hold us back. Malignant people missed the developmental stage where a conscience is formed; they have no internal limits on their behavior. The only limits they heed are external. They have to be stopped by a stronger outside force.

People with lesser personality disorders can be reasoned with, even convinced to change their ways. Malignants can't be rehabilitated: They have no remorse and no desire to change. They see their path as the only one, and they think that the rest of the human race is foolish to have feelings for others. Their lack of remorse persists even after they're exposed or sent to jail.

The best way to deal with malignant people is not to deal with them at all. Give them a very wide berth when you see them coming. Of course, the trick is to see them coming. The following are some symptoms of malignancy to look out for:

- **Someone who seems too good to be true.** People who are too perfect are probably hiding something. A malignant person will reveal no weaknesses. When he comes in for a job interview, he'll have an answer for everything; he won't stumble over his words or seem awkward or unsure of himself. The kind of effort it takes to come across as too-good-to-be-true is usually made only by someone with

evil intent. Real life is like running a marathon. Carrying out malignant scams is like sprinting—no one can keep it up forever.

- **Someone who always tells you what you want to hear.** Malignant people are incredibly seductive—they're shameless flatterers who know exactly what to say and when to say it. *Example:* When applying for the job, Terence noticed that Jack had a lower-class accent and sensed that he was insecure about his background and education. He reassured Jack by telling him that even though he, Terence, was from an upper-class background, he disliked effete intellectual snobs and really only respected "men of the people" like Jack.
- **An extremely negative history from somewhere.** The problem here is to comprehend that someone so charming, intelligent and accomplished could possibly have done such terrible things. This was Jack's problem when he got the negative information about Terence. Normal people tend to resolve cognitive dissonance by believing the malignant person. They rationalize what they've learned by telling themselves that everyone has a few bad traits. And they assume that whatever the problems are, they can handle them.
- **Your own failure to check references** because you've fallen under the person's spell. A malignant person can be very convincing about his past.
- **Ignoring signs of trouble.** Not only did Jack discount Terence's unreliability, but he failed to pay attention to the telephone call he overheard. Jack thought the notion of Terence using a company warehouse to store drugs too far-fetched, and he told himself he'd heard wrong. That was the crucial moment. Up until then, the malignancy could have been circumvented. But after that, Terence was like a cancerous growth. Jack never knew how much he'd lost until it was too late.

The malignant person is much more skilled than you are at dirty tricks. He's better at nastiness, dishonesty, even violence. He's sunk his fangs in more deeply than you know. And, unlike you, he has no scruples.

To counter a malignant person, you have to come on strong from an unexpected direction—exactly what Stormin' Norman Schwartzkopf did to Saddam Hussein.

Here is some advice:

- **Don't act out of impulse.** Think out your strategy.
- **Draw on all the people you trust,** including colleagues, friends and bosses. Check your plan with them, and enlist their advice and help. Also, consider hiring a lawyer.

- *Do the unexpected.* Malignant people count on you being an ordinary, predictable, law-abiding citizen whom they can steamroll. They don't count on a pincer attack. In Jack's case, he told a select group of friends and associates about his plight. They suggested that he pretend to cooperate with Terence while quietly going to his boss and the company's security officer. Both his boss and the security officer believed him. Together they set up a trap. Terence was caught red-handed in a warehouse with the cocaine. This plan succeeded because Terence never suspected that Jack was capable of any kind of covert action against him.

Empire-Building Bureaucrats

Empire-building bureaucrats are dangerous narcissists who burrow their way to the top. In the old Soviet system, the idea was to get a position and wait to inherit power by default. Soviet bureaucrats were weak on decision-making, but they had tyrannical control over vast populations. The weak rose to power by default, and eventually the empire crumbled.

Psychologist and consultant Knaus sees the same thing happening in this country. He says that in both state and corporate bureaucracies, the goal of upper administrators is to cover their tails, make things look good on the outside and say a lot without saying anything. These people are called managers, but they neither function like managers nor are competent to manage others.

Bureaucrats are experts at office politics. They are attracted to easy jobs where they can push papers around. Because they don't have anything of substance to do, they often get involved in various nonproductive office intrigues.

Empire builders are bureaucrats obsessed with power and control. They're threatened by competence, and they tend to find ways to discredit competent people. Like tyrants, they generally have very little empathy.

The goal of an empire-building administrator is to increase her power and authority by hiring more and more people who often do less and less work. These people try to look busy to justify their salaries. This substantially reduces efficiency. Empire-building bureaucrats will invariably try to hire friends and people who are beholden to them. They surround themselves with fawning sycophants who hope to inherit the same power at a later date.

Empire-building bureaucrats rely on their own cunning and on making things look good—keeping things quiet, not rocking the boat. They see themselves as stronger and better than other people. Because they're in positions of authority, they think they can get away with committing manipulative acts—even though their antics may appear ridiculous to the outside world.

The typical tactic of an empire-building bureaucrat is to build a paper trail against you. They use this tactic to assert power and control and to intimidate their employees; no one dares to say anything for fear the same thing will happen to him. They'll write up negative memos accusing you of various things that have little to do with your job. These memos are typically very vague, but they sound very official.

Most people don't answer the memos or gather evidence in support of their own positions because they assume—mistakenly—that no one would ever believe the accusations. So the paper trail builds and, eventually, the bureaucrat claims to have a stack of complaints against you that she then uses as justification to demote or fire you.

Observation: Paper trails are most likely to occur where there's a union or in the civil service, where a bureaucrat has to build a case against people to get rid of them. Many large corporations are also demanding massive documentation today before someone can be fired or demoted, however. So corporate bureaucrats also construct paper trails.

Example: James, the superintendent of a mental health institution, went after Vera, the head of the adolescent unit. She was out of favor because she'd criticized James' failure to apply for federal funding for her unit. Vera complained that James disseminated confidential information derived from her personnel file to people outside. In response, James turned around and had his internal affairs officer investigate her. The internal affairs officer found that there was no way of knowing exactly what had happened and that there was no basis for a complaint against her. James made sure no one knew about this report. Then another report surfaced, where the conclusion was that Vera had lied and fabricated evidence against the superintendent. She was demoted as a result.

When Vera sued, the matter was investigated by the state attorney general, who was aghast at James' duplicity. Document searches turned up the first report, which found Vera innocent. The second report was a 180-degree reversal of that verdict. Vera's mistake: She should have gathered information about James earlier in the game.

Observation: Many people don't react to a paper trail because it doesn't occur to them that each piece of paper will be used to build a case against them. It's important to counter *each* incident *as it occurs.*

Beating bureaucrats at their own game

Your best approach is to get facts and documentation. If an empire-builder makes accusations about you, respond to her with facts and information. *Goal:* Overwhelm her with information. You'll have to work hard at it, however, because there may be three or four people writing negative memos about you simultaneously. Empire-building bureaucrats will co-opt people and get them to write negative memos about you in order to fill a file. Most victims get overwhelmed by the sheer volume of charges they have to answer.

Here are some strategies that can help you avoid this kind of trap:

- *Investigate.* Take each negative memo, get the facts, talk to those involved and get statements and documentation that support you.
- *Respond effectively* in a well-constructed, nonemotional, factual way. The empire-building bureaucrat will have trouble dealing with that because she's used to being on the offensive, not the defensive.
- *Stay on guard.* After defending yourself, you may find that the empire-builder won't do anything for several weeks or months because she's trying to figure out how to handle the situation. Eventually, she will respond, and you may be in for a protracted battle.
- *Be prepared to file a grievance.* Find people who will support your version of events, and closely follow your company's grievance procedures. Before filing a grievance, Dr. Grothe recommends that you:
  - *Assess your case.* How strong is it? Get objective opinions.
  - *Document your case.* Carefully prepare the appropriate letters, previous appraisal forms, attendance records and witnesses.
  - *Be prepared for a case to be made against you.* Empire-building bureaucrats don't roll over and play dead. Prepare for an unfair fight, with personal attacks, mud-slinging and falsehoods.
  - *Be prepared to be outgunned.* Bosses often go into grievance procedures with the support of the entire organization. One company routinely has a company lawyer accompany bosses to grievance hearings, just to intimidate employees.
  - *Expect things to change dramatically after you file your grievance.* You may become the victim of cold shoulders or even outright retaliation.
  - *Be prepared to lose.* One study showed that 60 percent of grievances in a large institution failed.
  - *Don't give up.* It is possible to survive. You won't be popular with the empire-building bureaucrat and her claque, but you weren't popular to begin with.

You may ask yourself why you'd want to be involved in an organization that supports an empire-building bureaucrat. Some people are better off leaving overly bureaucratic organizations. But others are committed to the work they do, especially in nonprofit agencies in which people care deeply about those they're helping.

Unfortunately, nonprofits attract empire-building bureaucrats. They thrive in circumstances where there's no bottom line that can be used to judge them.

Petty Bureaucrats

Every office has at least one petty bureaucrat in a key position who serves as a roadblock to executives who want to get things done. Although empire-building bureaucrats will generally be higher up in the company, petty bureaucrats will often be at a fairly low level. Their lowly position in the hierarchy does not make them any easier to deal with, however. In fact, the reason they are petty is that they have fairly unimpressive jobs.

The petty bureaucrat is often an assistant—to the office manager, personnel director or department head. Petty bureaucrats may also be secretaries to high-level executives or supply-room managers. These employees are in indirectly powerful positions. They don't have the power to actually get something done, but they do have the power to prevent things from getting done. In fact, they can frustrate you until you're ready to scream.

Let's say your department needs another copy machine. You've noticed that the bookkeeping department upstairs has three copiers, one of which is almost never used. You ask the assistant office manager if you can have the extra copier. She demands a long memo explaining in excruciating detail why you need it, with a copy to the head of the bookkeeping department, who has to give his approval. Then, she has to send that memo in triplicate to your boss and his boss for approval. After they approve, a copy has to go to the head of the company, who happens to be in Argentina for the month and can't be reached because of a political upheaval. If you ever get the copy machine, you've already designated the half-hour a day you have to stand in line for copies as meditation time, and you're ready to join a Buddhist monastery.

Getting more than one pencil or pen at a time can be like pulling teeth if the head of the supply room is a petty bureaucrat. Sending a package FedEx instead of by fourth-class mail can be more trouble than it's worth if the mailroom head is a petty bureaucrat. It can be next to impossible to see your CEO in person if his secretary is a petty bureaucrat who guards his office like Cerberus at the gate of Hell.

Petty bureaucrats are trying to compensate for their lack of formal power within the organization. They have chips on their shoulders because they don't have the required combination of talent, intelligence, education and personality to get ahead.

In their hearts, they see themselves at the professional or executive level. Because they don't have what it takes for these positions, they need to assert power in the only way they can—by giving others, especially those who actually have the positions they want, the hardest time possible.

Many petty bureaucrats are unhappy in their personal lives as well. They're frustrated husbands, neglected wives or lonely singles who have no outlet for their feelings outside the office. They're angry and miserable, and they need to take it out on someone. If you're standing in front of their desk with a request they can frustrate, you become that someone.

Dealing with the petty bureaucrat

Going along with the petty bureaucrat's requests for multiple memos is obviously not the best approach. You can't play her game and win because that means waiting for what you need—or going to an absurd amount of trouble to get it.

Blowing up at the petty bureaucrat won't work either, even though that's the route most of us take out of sheer frustration. "What do you mean it's going to take three weeks to get a new chair?" you shriek. "If I have to sit on my chair for another day, I'm going to wind up in traction."

Making people lose their tempers is a victory for petty bureaucrats. They just love to see the high and mighty lose control. After you lose it, they'll just give you a self-satisfied sneer and reply, "It might take four weeks—depending on how long it takes me to fill out all the forms."

Going over the head of the petty bureaucrat might seem the obvious approach. Alas, it won't work. There is a reason the petty bureaucrat is where he is. Putting

petty bureaucrats in charge of departments like the mailroom, the phone system and the supply room saves money, even at the expense of everyone else's blood pressure. These people are rarely fired because they're wonderful scapegoats: Petty bureaucratic flunkies can be blamed for all the cheapness and evasiveness that really lies at the feet of top management.

There is one way and one way only to deal with petty bureaucrats: You must befriend them. Remember, they're insecure, self-hating, lonely misfits. They're desperate for a kind word or a smile. Of course, they're so defensive that they can't make the first move. And their sour, hateful attitude makes it highly unlikely that anyone will be friendly. Their nastiness breeds more nastiness in return and a vicious circle is the result. A kindly word or an expression of personal interest from an executive or a manager can perform miracles.

Use the following tips to soften up a petty bureaucrat:

- *Compliment his outfit;* inquire after his health; share a little office gossip. Draw the petty bureaucrat out and get him to talk about himself. Ask him how he feels about his job or the company.
- *Ask his advice.* If you know the petty bureaucrat has teenage children, you might tell him you're having a tough time with your teenage son and ask for some sympathy or advice. When he is all geared up to stymie your request for something he controls, this ploy can have some startling results. The petty bureaucrat will be enormously flattered that you would reveal something personal about yourself and ask the advice of someone on his level. You might get not only the sympathy you asked for but also that new chair you wanted the next day.

Observation: The people who befriend petty bureaucrats become office legends. Your reputation as someone who can get along with anyone will spread, and the effect on your career in general can only be positive.

Power Posturers

Power posturers assert their power in various ways. They may come late to meetings, sit in a certain spot in the room or wear the right designer clothes. They may drop names, interrupt you or make you sit in their offices and wait while they talk to someone else on the phone. Often, they grab credit for your accomplishments. Although they lord it over their subordinates, these people play up to the more powerful people in the company.

It may seem to subordinates that the power posturer holds all of the cards, but not according to psychologist Barry Lubetkin of the New York Institute for Behavior Therapy. He says, "There is a downside to power. Power posturers attract an enormous amount of hostility. Superficially their subordinates may seem to be compliant and worshipful, but secretly they will undercut and sabotage the power posturer as much as they can get away with."

How much the power posturer is resented will depend on how much his subordinates think he deserves his power. So if a power player really holds a high position, he can get away with more power posturing. A CEO can make employees wait to see him without garnering too much resentment. But beware the middle manager who makes his department heads cool their heels for too long. He may be in for a lot of nasty gossip and potential sabotage.

The other price of power posturing may be internal. Some people think power posturing is the only way to get ahead. They're not power players by nature. But they read or hear so much about how to win through intimidation that they start adopting behaviors they may not *really* be comfortable with.

"It takes a lot of effort to act powerful," Dr. Lubetkin says. "It takes effort to come late to a meeting, to seat yourself in the power position in the room, to interrupt someone when he's making a presentation, just to assert your power. Because most human beings would ultimately like others to approve of them, the person who's engaging in power posturing is likely to feel some dissonance inside himself between his behavior and the way he feels he should be acting.

"For example, I see chief execs or middle-management types who have learned how to act powerful. They learn where to sit, to keep others waiting, to draw attention to themselves, and so on. But it's an act—it's a well-developed, well-thought-out act—and it's inconsistent with the way they really want to be. So they feel like phonies and may wind up depressed. They may also wind up with stress-related illnesses like heart disease, asthma or high blood pressure."

The main thing to remember is that the power posturer is insecure and doesn't really feel worthy of the power she has acquired. To deal with the power posturer, you have to do an end run around the posturing and try to appeal to the real person inside.

If the power posturer is a fairly benign type, whose posturing just consists of wearing the latest designer clothes or dropping the names of movie stars or political figures, don't burst his bubble. Power posturers will bear lifelong grudges against people who have the audacity to point out the posturers' self-importance. Instead, take a deep breath and compliment the Armani jacket and listen reverently to the tale of the evening spent with Senator whoever. Then bring up whatever issue is important to you. You'll have softened up the power posturer by feeding his self-importance. He'll feel grateful and want to help you.

Resist being intimidated by the more manipulative power posturer. This type will interrupt, keep you waiting while he talks on the phone, seat you on a tiny, uncomfortable chair while he sits in a huge recliner or denigrate you. Don't accept such treatment. If you let the power posturer intimidate you, he'll hold you in contempt, and you'll get nowhere. Here's how to resist intimidation:

- *If he's making you wait* in his office while he's on the phone or busy with someone else, get up and leave. Tell him to call you when he's ready to give you some time alone. If his secretary is making you wait, tell her the same thing.
- *If he interrupts,* keep on talking until you can get him to be quiet.
- *Keep your cool.* If the power posturer is trying to pressure you into something, keep repeating that you understand what he's talking about, but you see it differently. Acknowledge that you don't have his decision-making authority, but you do know your area of expertise and must dissent.
- *Demand respect* from the power posturer and you'll get it. *Good statement:* "I've always done good work, and in order to continue to do good work, I need to be in an atmosphere where people respect me."
- *Do a little power posturing of your own.* The power posturer is insecure. If you look down your nose at him in an area where you're the expert and he isn't, he'll respect you more.

Are you a power posturer?

Many executives do a lot of unconscious power posturing. How do you know if it's *your* problem? Ask yourself these questions:

- Am I comfortable with power?
- How comfortable am I exercising power? Does it upset me? Do I find it exhausting? To answer these questions, review the last five things you did that communicated power or authority to others.
- Is there a discrepancy between my home life and my work life? Am I always posturing? All powerful people need a refuge, a place to get out of the pressure

cooker. Home is supposed to be that place. If your home doesn't provide such relief, you have to rethink the nature of your relationships and stop running your home life the way you run your business.

You can cure yourself of power posturing. Take the following steps:

- **Be honest with people.** Tell people the truth about how you feel. Dishonesty is often one of the prices of power. Fight this trend by saying what you really feel about an issue or a person—and how you feel about yourself.
- **Learn how to back off.** Learn how to apologize sincerely. If you keep someone waiting, apologize. Then ask yourself, "Did I really mean that, or am I being phony?"
- **Recognize that you don't have to demonstrate your power at every moment.** Just because you ease up for a while—show up on time, take the weakest position at a meeting or give total credit to someone else—it won't destroy your position within the organization. Power posturers are terrified of letting down their guard—they think one chink in their armor will destroy them.

Recommendation: Look to the powerful people you know in your own organization. How do these people behave? What do they say? How do their actions make you respect them rather than scorn them? Chances are, they don't posture.

Sexual Harassers

Sexual harassment has been a reality in the workplace since men and women began working together. However, only recently has it been considered a problem. Women used to have to "put up with" inappropriate comments and behavior, or risk damage to their careers. Some gave in to their pursuers; most simply found new jobs as soon as they could. However, now that the law has caught up with reality, victims of sexual harassment have the means—and even the obligation—to demand equal respect and consideration on the job.

Men who just don't get it

Many sexual harassers are not deliberately trying to intimidate or seduce the women they work with—they simply don't get it. Whether they were raised to treat women differently or raised by wolves, they somehow never got the message that sexual innuendo, endearments and intimate touching have no place in the workplace.

These men are not necessarily trying to have sexual relationships with their female employees and co-workers. They act flirtatious with all the women around them—family members, friends and neighbors. If you get angry with them, they'll act hurt and say, "But I didn't mean anything by it." They sincerely believe they can't cause any distress unless they consciously intend to. There are a number of ways to deal with men who don't "get it":

- **Educate them.** Often, a man who behaves inappropriately with women as a rule will respond to clear, rational education. Simply let him know the rules have changed. Sit down with the offender, and in a friendly, nonthreatening way, explain that his behavior is making the women around him uncomfortable. Because this is exactly the opposite of what he's trying to do, you should get his attention. Give examples of behavior that crosses the line—hugging, back rubs, sexual remarks and so forth. Don't name names or put him on the defensive. Gently lead him to the natural conclusion that the right way to impress and work well with his female colleagues and staff is to treat them with the same dignity and respect he gives male workers.

Observation: If your boss is the harasser, you need to ask yourself if he's likely to respond well to this approach. Your goal is to put an end to the harassment. If talking to him directly is likely to work, give it a try. However, if there's a chance he still won't "get it"—or could react negatively—you may want to take a more formal tack. Going through your company's established sexual harassment reporting procedure may offer greater job protection in case your boss tries to retaliate against you because of your accusations.

- **Try humor.** With some men, a humorous or sarcastic remark will work, especially if the man is a secure person with a good sense of humor. Sexual jokes and innuendo are often used by men to "initiate" new members into their group. Responding with a well-timed jab can establish your place in the group and move your relationship past this testing stage.

Caution: A sarcastic remark may backfire if the offender is insecure or lacks a sense of humor. If you think he may "dish it out better than he takes it," consider approaching someone who knows him better and asking for help. You don't have to plead—just mention in passing that you wish Bob didn't make so many sexual comments. Say, "You're closer to him than I am. Maybe you could say something. It's really starting to interfere with my ability to work with him."

Heavy-duty harassers

Although you can often deal directly with men who don't intend to offend, heavy-duty harassers can cause serious harm to your self-esteem and your career. With these types, offensive behavior isn't about sex, it's about gaining and maintaining power. Heavy-duty harassers need to prove themselves by conquering their targets—often by intimidating them constantly until they break down and submit, or leave.

Heavy-duty harassers damage their companies as well as their victims. The legal penalties for sexual har-assment are severe; juries now routinely bring in multimillion-dollar awards for injured plaintiffs. Those judgments are usually assessed against the employer rather than the offender, especially if the sexual harasser was in a position of authority or had a known history of inappropriate behavior. Companies want and need to know if someone in their employ is putting the organization at risk of legal action. Here are some strategies for dealing with heavy-duty harassers:

- *Document and confront.* If you want to stop the harassment without necessarily filing a lawsuit, consider presenting the "evidence" directly to the offender. Dr. Grothe brings up the example of Elizabeth, a staff writer for a national magazine, who was being harassed by her editor, Maurice. Elizabeth wrote down each instance of harassment in a notebook with dates, times and places. She also carried a small tape recorder with her and surreptitiously tape-recorded his propositions. Eventually, Elizabeth sent Maurice a long, formal letter and a copy of the tape. She documented what he'd done, talked about the emotional distress it caused her, and told him to stop or she would file a grievance with the EEOC for sexual harassment, sue the company, and send a copy of the tape to his wife. She added that if he stopped voluntarily, she'd let bygones be bygones. From that moment on, Maurice was a changed man—at least around Elizabeth.

This approach has two advantages: (1) It often succeeds in bringing the harassment to an end; and (2) it gives the victim a sense of power over the harasser. Collecting data, updating records and anticipating the final assault empowers you in the face of the bully's repeated attempts to humiliate. Your victory will indeed be sweet.

- *Go over the harasser's head.* If you can't overpower the offender with your evidence, consider taking it to someone who has power over him. But be careful. Leapfrogging the wrong person can be dangerous,

especially if there's something you don't know. "I made the mistake once," Dr. Grothe relates, "of telling a woman who was being sexually harassed by her boss that she should talk to her boss's boss. She did that. But her boss's boss was having an affair with his secretary, and he really took the view that if she didn't dress and act provocatively, her boss would never have come on to her. After a few months, my client had to leave her job. I felt guilty because I had, in my naiveté, given her advice I thought was appropriate."

Make sure the person you approach can be trusted to act in the company's best interests. If you do find just the right person to make the complaint to, the results can be very satisfying. *Example:* Harriet worked in a bank where Herb, a middle-level manager, had a history of having affairs with the female employees. He was putting pressure on Harriet to sleep with him, intimating that he could make life very difficult for her if she did not. Harriet knew that Herb's boss and Herb were squash partners and that she wasn't likely to have any luck going to him. Finally she found Lydia, a new bank vice president who was a person of strength, conviction and moral integrity. Lydia, who was well-established with a strong power base, was one of the protégées of the bank president. Harriet told Lydia about the pressure Herb had been putting on her, and also about all of the other escapades Herb had been guilty of over the last couple of years. She said his harassing behavior had been ignored by company higher-ups.

Lydia had the choice of taking formal action against Herb or using the informal approach. She chose the informal. She took Herb out to lunch, looked him straight in the eye and said, "I know exactly what you're doing with Harriet now, and I know what you've done over the last couple of years. I don't care what you do in your personal life. If you want to go to bars after work and chase women, that's fine. But if you ever do it here in this organization again, I am going to make sure you're run out." She scared the daylights out of Herb. He never bothered Harriet again and his behavior, although it probably didn't change outside the organization, changed dramatically within it.

- *File a formal charge.* If direct measures aren't likely to work or have already failed to stop the harassment, you can always file a grievance with the EEOC, hire a lawyer and threaten to sue. Don't expect it to be easy. The legal process can be lengthy and invasive, and it has a way of developing a life of its own.

Proving harassment in a court of law, to a government agency, an administrative law judge, an arbitrator or even your company's sexual harassment prevention team can be difficult and disconcerting. Your personal life may be scrutinized; your own behavior brought into question. Don't expect companywide support for your action, either.

Many women who file sexual harassment complaints are seen as traitors within the organization, whistleblowers or, at the very least, certainly not "team players." Even if you win the case, you may lose the confidence and camaraderie you once enjoyed with your other male colleagues. Nevertheless, if you're the victim of sexual harassment (and men can be sexually harassed as well), you have every right and even the duty to take whatever action is necessary to bring the problem to an end. The offender's behavior is not only causing you discomfort, but it's hurting others in the organization and it's definitely putting the company at serious risk.

This is not an issue to be taken lightly, dismissed or swept under the rug. Sexual harassment in any form must be confronted and fully redressed.

Indirect Aggressors

2

Indirect aggressors, or "passive-aggressives" as they are labeled by psychologists, seem to be very agreeable on the surface. They seem to be cooperative; they always say yes. But they have an enormous capacity to thwart you when they choose.

Passive-aggressives express their aggression in indirect ways—thus, their name. They never come right out and tell you what's bothering them, and they almost never get visibly angry. They sneak up on you instead. They do things that can be excused or justified, such as having accidents, forgetting or missing the point.

People who use this kind of indirect aggression are quite self-centered. They are unable to sympathize with the motivations and feelings of others, and they feel entitled to have things their own way. But they are afraid of direct conflict. If you complain about their behavior, they turn things around so it looks as though it's your fault. Passive-aggressives share traits with more blatantly aggressive people: They manipulate, intrude and exploit when it suits their ends. Because of their fear of direct conflict, however, they use methods that they hope you won't discover. Here are some examples:

- You're angry because Joe has handed in his marketing survey three days after you promised it to your client. Joe is standing at your desk with an expression of total innocence, saying, "But you said it was OK to hand it in today." If Joe is convincing enough, you may start to wonder if you actually did tell him it was all right to hand it in today.
- You're supervising Tessa, a sales representative, who seems to be knowledgeable, personable, aggressive and a good closer. But, for some reason, she isn't making as many sales as she ought to. Something always goes wrong. Tessa is about to approach a key prospect whose business the company really wants. You go over her presentation item by item, attending to every detail, but she fails to make the sale. When you ask her what happened, she says the customer wanted delivery by June, and she couldn't promise it sooner than August. You blow up, saying, "What do you mean August?! We could have gotten it to him by May." Tessa replies, "Why didn't you tell me that in the first place?" You're left steaming.

- You lend a co-worker an important file, and he promises to bring it back in an hour. Three days later, you go to his office looking for it and it's nowhere to be found. He says he mislaid it and apologizes profusely, but you wonder. You know he felt resentful when you got promoted over him, even though he never said anything about it.
- You're at a business lunch with your boss and other members of the company. After the meal, you order dessert. Alice, a friend and colleague in whom you confided your concerns about your weight because you thought she was sympathetic, says loudly, "You shouldn't eat that; you're supposed to be on a diet." When you later confront her about embarrassing you in public, she says, "But I was only trying to help you not gain any weight."

Passive aggression is essentially a self-centered, rebellious kind of behavior that defies direction or control. Thus, it's very similar to the behavior of children from the ages of about 8 to 12. Children in that age group are going through a stage called latency. They may be rebellious, but, unlike older adolescents, they are usually afraid to be directly confrontational. Instead, they'll "yes" you to death and then do whatever they please. They are aware of the expectations of others, but they have no interest in meeting them.

If you're having trouble identifying a colleague's actions as passive-aggressive, ask yourself if they resemble a 12-year-old's behavior.

Example: After the sixth time you ask your child to take out the trash—his regularly assigned chore—he finally grabs hold of the bag grudgingly, lifts it wrong end up, and spills its contents all over your morning newspaper.

Adult passive-aggressives are very frustrating people. But, just like kids, they can be very lovely and cooperative if they're doing what they want to do. And that's your first cue to handling them: Never exert too much control, or they'll get rebellious. The following are some tips for confronting passive-aggressive people:

- ***Don't get defensive or angry.*** Passive-aggressives feed on the anger of others. When confronted, they will only get worse. The more you try to control their indirect aggression, the more they tend to screw up.

- *Point out unacceptable behavior and explain why it has to improve.* Get the person's suggestions about what he thinks he can do to improve the situation.
- *Don't accept excuses.* If the passive-aggressive claims the screw-up wasn't her fault or her responsibility, stress that she has to be accountable. *Example:* When Tessa blamed her boss for not telling her about delivery dates, the boss should have replied, "Whether I told you or not, finding out about those dates was your responsibility."
- *Don't put yourself in a position of dependency.* You can't depend on passive-aggressives. They won't come through when you really need them.

Observation: Passive-aggressives do best when given limited direction and a lot of autonomy. Because of their innate rebelliousness, they make terrible team members.

The passive-aggressive boss

If you're unlucky enough to work for a passive-aggressive boss—and many of us are—the trick is to be extremely cautious. Don't presume anything or take anything for granted. Be ultracorrect. Carefully stay within the guidelines and rules; being creative and adventurous could give him an opportunity to stab you in the back. Get everything in writing. *The favorite sentence of the passive-aggressive:* "I never said that."

If you don't know your boss really well, study him. Do exit interviews with his victims, and talk to the wise old hands at the office to get their advice. To avoid his trigger points, do a lot of careful negotiating around anything important. Again, make no assumptions; write down what you agree on, and run that agreement by him before you leave ("Just to be sure I've got it all straight....")

Different kinds of passive-aggressives pose different kinds of problems. In this section, we describe the various types of passive-aggressives and offer tactics tailored to deal with each one.

Button Pushers

Most of us have two or three sensitive areas—soft spots where we're vulnerable and others can manipulate us. When people push those buttons, we go into an automatic response pattern. Those are the areas where we keep getting manipulated. If you know where your problem areas are, you can take protective measures to keep button pushers from getting to you.

There are a lot of button pushers around. They never ask you outright for anything, of course. Before you know it, however, you are doing their bidding and asking yourself, "How did I get into this one?"

All of us have done a little button pushing at one time or another, or we wouldn't be human. As kids, we were experts at knowing what Mom's weaknesses were and exploiting them. When we wanted to stay home from school, we knew how to look really sick and pitiful. In most families, however, there was also a system of direct communication that enabled children to get what they wanted by asking for it.

But if someone comes from the kind of family where they can only get what they want through indirection—by finding and pushing their parents' buttons—chances are they'll grow up to be button pushers. They'll automatically go for what they want by sensing and exploiting the weaknesses of others.

How do you know when someone's pushing your buttons? Most people know that they're being manipulated when they feel uncomfortable and don't know the reason why. You might feel anxious, pushed around, angry or overly compliant when you're with a button pusher. You may resist seeing this person, try too hard to please him or steer the conversation away from important topics. Work on increasing your self-awareness to avoid being manipulated by button pushers.

The following list of the most common buttons comes from Dr. Marlin Potash, author of *Hidden Agendas: What's Really Going on in Your Relationships—in Love, at Work, in Your Family* (Dell).

- *People pleasing.* If you feel that people will like you only if you please and accommodate them, you're in big trouble. You'll do almost anything others want to make them happy. And button pushers know this; as a result, count on them to say things like, "I know I can count on you... I don't know what I'd do without you," to get you to do their bidding.
- *Fear of conflict.* If you're afraid of others' anger, the button pusher will threaten to have a tantrum. *Tipoff button-pusher phrases:* "Let me make my position perfectly clear..."; "If you don't like it, speak up now..."; "I don't want to start an argument, but...."
- *Need for acceptance.* If you have to fit in with the crowd, you're prey for the button pusher who threatens to embarrass you. *Tipoff button-pusher phrases:* "Everyone I've spoken to agrees that..."; "I know what a team player you are..."; "As I'm sure you know...."

- *Discomfort with silence.* If you feel rejected or disapproved of by people who don't respond to you, you're at the mercy of button pushers who wait for your response, sulk, stare you down, never crack a smile or ignore you.
- *Perfectionism.* If you have to do everything perfectly, and if you tend to take on more than you can handle, you'll be vulnerable to intimations that you can't handle a particular task. *Tipoff phrases:* "Maybe I'm asking too much of you, but..."; "It isn't how I would have handled it, but..."; "You look tired; are you spreading yourself too thin?"
- *Competitiveness.* If you love to win and hate to lose, you're an easy mark for invidious comparisons. *Tipoff phrases:* "The person who had this job before you..."; "You're the only one on my staff who doesn't..."; "Harry finds time to...."
- *A short temper.* If you're easily angered, a button pusher can set you off by needling you, teasing you or embarrassing you. The button pusher will find out what gets you going. Then, after you blow up, he plays the role of the injured party. *Tipoff phrases:* "What did I do to deserve that?" "You're too sensitive; I was only joking."
- *Being a sucker for flattery.* We all love a compliment, but some of us are so insecure that we're overly grateful for praise or recognition. We feel we have to repay it. *Tipoff phrases:* "I know it's asking a lot, but only you can do this job." "You're the only one I trust."

Psychologist Barry Lubetkin recommends the following strategies to resist manipulation:

- *Say the four magic words: "I need more time."* Most people get manipulated because they get overwhelmed. They succumb to the time pressure the manipulator is putting on them to make a quick decision. Recognize that one of your inalienable human rights is to stall. Give yourself time to reflect on what decision you ultimately want to make.
- *Understand where the button pusher is coming from.* Some people are manipulative because they feel threatened or powerless. These types have gone to the other extreme. They have learned to be dishonest in an effort to overcompensate. Or they've come from a manipulative family, as we mentioned earlier. Understanding won't make you less vulnerable, but it will make you less angry. That, in turn, will make it easier to think of a way to deal with this situation.
- *Try "fogging."* This is a psychological term that means agreeing in principle with the truth of what the manipulator says in order to outmanipulate him. *Example:* Your boss tries to pressure you into doing a job you don't want to do by saying that you're the only one who can handle it. You agree, saying, "Yes, I probably would be the best choice for the job. But I can't do it right now." So to outfox the manipulator, always agree in principle, but keep repeating your refusal to go along with his request.
- *Question the person.* Reveal your feeling that you're being manipulated via a question. *Example:* Your boss tries to get you to agree with him by saying, "I know you'll do this because you're a real team player." You respond innocently, "Are you trying to pressure me into this decision?"
- *Use a humorous remark:* Deflect the manipulation with humor. *Examples:* "You wouldn't be trying to guilt-trip me into this, would you?" "If I'm that indispensable, maybe I should ask for a raise."
- *Agree to what the button pusher wants, but let him know you're on to him.* *Example:* "Sure I'll do that for you, but don't think I fell for your hard-luck story."

Putdown Artists

"It took you a whole month to do this?" "This office looks really nice the way you fixed it up. Don't get too used to it." "I can't believe I hired you."

Verbal zaps and zingers are like sandpaper rubbing slowly across your sense of self—eventually your self-esteem wears away. Putdowns are often so much a part of our daily lives that we hardly notice them until we start feeling depressed without knowing why.

But if you work for a putdown artist or with verbally abusive colleagues, you'll start dreading coming into the office after a while. At first, you may tell yourself you're just being too sensitive, that you shouldn't take it personally. But let's face it: Those comments draw blood. After enough of them, you may be ready to quit to get out of the line of fire.

Unless you're dealing with an out-and-out sadist, however, don't give up so quickly. There are many effective ways to deal with putdown artists. First, you need to understand them.

Putdown artists are usually perfectionists. They were constantly criticized as children and ended up believing that love and approval come only to those who are perfect. But you can only be "perfect" by comparison. So, perfectionists tend to put others down to boost themselves up.

Perfectionists also have the mistaken notion that high levels of dissatisfaction or complaining about others' behavior will improve that behavior. But even though verbal putdowns are an accepted part of our culture, positive reinforcement—not negativity—creates more energy. Encouragement helps both children and adults far more than criticism.

The first step in self-defense is recognizing that you've been attacked, however subtly. *Signs:* A queasy feeling in your stomach or a depressed feeling after a conversation. Once you know you've been hurt, it's never too late to set up a defense. These tactics were suggested by Dr. Jennifer James, author of *You Know I Wouldn't Say This If I Didn't Love You* (Newmarket Press):

- **Agree with everything the sniper says, if you have a sense of humor.** This works especially well with people who are either so dense that nothing else gets to them or who have a sense of humor themselves. *Putdown:* "Are you sure you spoke with the sales department before you wrote down these sales figures? They don't look right to me." *Reply:* "Sales department? Is that on the third floor? Why would I speak to them? They don't actually have any sales figures, do they?"

  The final remark after you've used this technique will probably be, "It just doesn't do any good to talk to you." That's your cue to respond, "Of course it doesn't, I'm just impossible."

- **Show no interest.** Blink your eyes, yawn or look away. Lack of interest is a great way to modify negative behavior. People hate to think that they're boring—especially when they were hoping to get a reaction.

- **Register the hit.** When hit by a nasty remark, act like the damage is physical. *Suggestion:* Put your hand up and say, "Ooh, something hit me; I wonder what it was?" and go on with the conversation. This is a signal that you're not easy prey. It will stop almost everyone except the worst offenders.

- **Analyze the remark.** Divide an attack into its parts and respond to each of them, without putting yourself into the position of aggrieved victim. *Putdown:* "Even a woman should be able to understand this." *Reply:* "When did you start thinking women were inferior?"

- **Send it back.** Acknowledge that you've been hit and confront it directly. *Good replies:* "I'm sure you didn't mean to insult me." "Is there any reason you would want to hurt my feelings?" "Are you

aware how that remark would sound to some people?" *Alternate strategy:* Ask the person what she meant by her nasty remark. If the putdown artist replies that she is only being honest, or is trying to help you, explain that you're an adult and prefer to get help in ways that don't hurt your feelings.

- **Keep a record.** Begin a list today, and track where the barbs are coming from. Give them a rating from one to 10. Which hurt the most? Just writing them down will give you perspective. It will also give you practice in identifying the worst offenders and a chance to think up advance strategies.

Learning from putdowns

Negative comments can give you important feedback. Many executives aren't sophisticated or skilled in communication. You only find out what others really think of you when they throw zingers your way. Use the following strategies to make the most of what you learn:

- **Avoid being defensive.** This is extremely tough. Set your feelings aside, and realize that in some way you're getting information about your work that you need to hear.

- **Check your self-esteem.** Ask yourself, "Why is this person able to make me feel bad so easily?"

- **Check the source.** Is this someone you have to listen to? Is he your boss or just a co-worker?

- **Get enough information.** Often we feel so devastated that we'll hear the remark, but we won't really understand what the person is talking about. *Good questions to ask:* "What do you mean? Where should I improve?" "In what area was the conference badly organized?"

- **Ask for help.** If this person is upset, the best way to cool her down is to ask for a suggestion on how to fix the complaint.

- **Prioritize.** Based on what was said, figure out what was important and what wasn't. We often give priority to something personal, like criticism of our looks, when the most important part of the conversation is a piece of technical information.

- **Decide what you're willing to do.** Are you willing to fix the problem? Can it be fixed? Is this person asking for too much? Is she just humiliating you?

- **Respond.** Don't tuck the putdown away or take it home and let it keep you up at night. A response—especially one that's not defensive—will gain you more respect.

Saboteurs

Saboteurs try to undermine your career or your self-confidence. They want what you have, and they are often willing to go to great lengths to get it.

Dr. Michael Zey, author of *Winning With People* (Tarcher), says that many saboteurs are what he calls *friendly enemies*. They give with one hand and take away with the other. *Example:* The colleague who is supportive, helpful and encouraging until you actually get that raise or promotion. Then, all of a sudden, she starts subtly undermining your self-confidence and questioning your abilities. These types are masters of the left-handed compliment. *Typical comment:* "How wonderful that you're getting a chance to work on the company's new desktop publishing venture. I didn't think you knew anything about computers."

Another type of saboteur is the backstabber. This individual does his work behind the scenes. The backstabber may have it in for you for reasons that you're not even aware of, and you only find out about it when negative things start happening. *Example:* After a brilliant career at her firm, a lawyer was passed over for a partnership, which she'd fully expected to get. She had no idea what had happened, and no one would tell her. Then the partner whom she worked for let slip that he knew she had applied for a job at another firm. There was no way he could have known that unless someone else had told him. The lawyer racked her brain, but couldn't think who could have told him or how this might have happened.

Months later, it came out that a paralegal, someone she barely knew, had been caught rifling through people's desks after work. The lawyer determined that the paralegal must have gone through her desk and found a copy of the letter she had written to the other firm and left it on her boss's desk. In this case, the paralegal who did it was simply a vengeful person who wanted to harm others who were more successful than himself.

In some cases, the saboteur has it in for you personally—you're rivals, or he just doesn't like you. In others, like the above example, there is no personal element involved. In still others, you just happen to be in the wrong place. Sometimes, the backstabber may be trying to promote her favorite over you for a particular position. You may find out you're the target of her attention when she begins to circulate negative "facts" about you. Or you may find yourself excluded from key meetings or projects. In other cases, you're attacked to hurt someone else—your boss, for example, who is the saboteur's rival.

According to Dr. Zey, saboteurs have a number of motives, such as:

- ***They want to get ahead.*** They may simply want your position and need to get you out of the way. This kind of sabotage is usually subtle. The saboteur will be friendly until you seem to be standing in her way. Then she'll withdraw her support or undermine you.
- ***They don't want anyone else to do well.*** This type of saboteur is resentful. She may lack a degree or needed experience in a particular field, and she believes she's gone as far as she can go. It bothers her that others are getting ahead.
- ***They don't like you.*** You may have insulted someone without knowing it, or you may remind the person of a hated parent or an ex-spouse. If the saboteur dislikes you for unconscious reasons, you may be in for it. In this case, there is no way to figure out what the person has to gain.
- ***They see you as a loser.*** Some people may have a low opinion of your abilities. They see you as incompetent. You may have some emotional or physical defect, such as stuttering or coming across as too self-effacing or insecure. If you value these saboteurs' opinions, their lack of faith in you will weaken your resolve and lower your chances for success.

How sabotage manifests itself

Sabotage may come from bosses, subordinates or peers. A boss may sabotage you by taking credit for your work, giving you a job you're not trained to do or assigning something that is at odds with your talents. *Example*: An editor gave a very overweight, obviously out-of-shape writer an assignment to report on the culture of CrossFit. She expected the writer to be too embarrassed to do well. But the writer overcame the sabotage by approaching the assignment with a sense of humor. When the people she was interviewing looked at her strangely, she joked about how sending her to a CrossFit workout was like sending a gourmet to report on a fast-food convention. This loosened up her interview subjects, and she got some good quotes.

The most insidious form of sabotage is from below. Subordinates can't express resentment openly; they passively undermine you, which makes this type of sabotage difficult to overcome. Subordinates may cause delays in a project, distort what you say when repeating it to others or leave out critical facts you need to know. They may "lose" critical material, be unavailable when needed or use a host of other passive-aggressive maneuvers. Their gossip is especially insidious. You will probably never get an opportunity to counter their malicious rumors—especially those spread in social situations, during lunch and at the water-cooler.

Here are the situations when sabotage is most likely:
- When you're new on the job and considered an outsider.
- When you're replacing a beloved boss.
- When you've been promoted and are supervising your former peers.
- When you're put in charge of the person everyone feels should have gotten the job instead of you.

Never ignore sabotage. It could cost you your career. Instead, deal with it in the following ways:

- *Get information.* Develop a good network of people who support you and tell you what's going on with your subordinates. Make sure you trust them to tell you the truth.
- *Get support.* Enlist the help of your support network to defeat the saboteur. *How:* If necessary, ask your supporters to talk to the saboteur or his or her supervisor. If nasty rumors are being spread about you, have your supporters counter them.
- *Confront the saboteur.* This is a delicate process, but it can work. *Crucial:* Have all the facts about the sabotage, and be sure that key members of the organization support you. Do it in private so there's no open battle. You may not be able to prove anything, but you will be putting the saboteur on notice that you know what he's up to and are prepared to defend yourself.
- *Pay attention to your gut feelings.* After being sabotaged, many people will say, "I had a hunch he was out to get me. I just didn't believe my intuition." If you're getting uneasy feelings about someone who seems to be friendly, trust your feelings. Our intuition is a sure-fire early warning system that we ignore at our peril.

Undercover Operators

The undercover operator has a hidden agenda that fouls up your relationship. The undercover operator may not even be aware of what's bothering him about you, but you get hints that something is awry.

According to Dr. Potash, the undercover operator may be the co-worker who's always smiling at you and telling you how much he loves working with you. You have lunch and share ideas. But something seems wrong: You get this funny, creepy feeling that this person isn't really your friend.

Or you may have a boss who is unfriendly, even though he doesn't find fault with your work. You see him smile and chat with other employees, but never with you. You know he has something against you, but you don't know what it is. Or you may have had a relationship with someone at work that was once open and friendly. Now that person has started to snub you. *Examples:* She goes out to lunch with others and does not ask you. She doesn't stop by your office anymore.

In many cultures, being direct and straightforward is unacceptable, especially if people have something negative to say. In almost all families, there are topics that are verboten. Forbidden topics are often about things the family imagines are shameful or hurtful. Therefore, when something bothers us about another person, telling that person the truth is the last thing that usually occurs to us.

This tendency toward secretiveness creates hidden agendas, where people act one way, but feel another. Undercover operators imagine that if they tell someone what's bothering them, some kind of disaster will occur. They've been so indoctrinated against coming right out with things that they keep secrets as a matter of course. But their refusal to be direct creates hurt, bafflement and confusion in their subordinates and co-workers.

If you feel that someone has a hidden agenda aimed against you, trust your judgment. Most of us automatically reject intuitive feelings about people because we've been taught to think rationally. If your intuition is telling you something is wrong, don't ignore it. In personal relationships, hunches and gut feelings are often as accurate as statistics. The only thing that's likely to be inaccurate is your reading of what's going on. We tend to project the things that bother us onto others, and we're often quite wrong. The only way to find out what the undercover operator is really thinking is to ask her.

Sometimes the truth can be something you wouldn't ever have imagined. *Example:* Ruth joined the marketing department of a large corporation, where Ann was already working. Because they shared a number of qualities, they gravitated toward each other and became lunch partners. Then, Mary joined the department, and Ann dropped Ruth like a hot potato. She started going to lunch regularly with Mary and wouldn't even talk to Ruth in the hall. Ruth felt terribly hurt by the rejection, and she couldn't imagine what she'd done wrong. She imagined all the possible ways in which she could have insulted or alienated Ann.

Ruth worked up her courage and insisted that Ann go out to lunch with her to talk. Ann admitted that she'd had to choose between friendship with Ruth or Mary. Mary was a very jealous person, who felt comfortable having only one close friend. Ann chose Mary because she did not want to lose her friendship. Ruth was stunned that someone could feel this way, but she was glad she'd found out the truth.

You have to confront the undercover operator. There's no other way. You can't read his mind. *Suggested statement:* "I don't know what's going on, but something is, and I would like to know what it is." *Add a few possibilities:* "Do you want my job?" "Are you upset that I got the promotion you didn't get?" "Are you afraid that I'll get to head up the new department over you?"

At this point, the undercover operator will probably vehemently deny any hidden agenda. However, unless the undercover operator is a very good actor, he will let something slip. You will get some idea of what the problem is, even though the other person won't admit it.

Dr. Potash gives an example from her own experience: "I had a boss once who used to get this look on his face after a meeting, like someone had just stabbed his mother—generally after I'd done a piece of really terrific work. Once I backed him into an elevator and said, 'Tony, I don't know what the problem is here, but every time I do a good piece of work your voice says good work, but the look on your face says, I'm really angry about something. I don't understand what the problem is.'

"He kept on protesting that there wasn't any problem, but I wouldn't give up. 'I'm not foolish,' I said. 'I wish you'd tell me what the problem is so I could do something about it. I come away from these meetings feeling I've done something wrong and I don't know what it is.' He harumphed and harumphed and denied everything. But as he continued harumphing from the 25th to the 1st floor, it clicked. I said, 'I work for you, and you're jealous that I'm doing good work, aren't you?'

"I'm not jealous," he said with an incredible overreaction. When someone overreacts, you know you've hit a nerve. I said, 'Are you concerned I'm going to take credit for these things instead of crediting you?' From the expression on his face, I could tell I'd hit the nail on the head. So I said, 'Tony, I work for you; you're my boss. Anything I do that's good reflects well on you, and I would never say anything but that. I always preface anything I do with how terrific it was that you let me work on the project, or what a great contribution you made. Your name is on every article I write. I'm not after your job, and I wouldn't get it if I were because I'm not qualified.'

"The confrontation helped. Tony felt better because he knew I wasn't after his job. He knew that when I did good work, I would credit him. As long as I mentioned his name first, everything worked out OK. Tony's hidden agenda was hard to ferret out," Dr. Potash adds, "because even he was unaware of what it was, which was to discredit me. He was doing it in an automatic way."

Here are some other helpful tactics:

- *Don't assume others view the world the way you do.* Dr. Potash says, "Getting credit was something that bothered Tony, and he assumed the same thing would bother me, so he couldn't ask for it outright. But I couldn't have cared less about giving him credit. For me, that was a transitional job, but it was his life's work."

- *Try to view the situation from other perspectives.* Ask yourself: "What could possibly bother another person here?" Don't make it an accusation instead of a question, as in, "Nothing I've done could possibly bother anybody." Something is bothering somebody if they're using a hidden agenda.

- *Ask probing questions* when trying to find out the undercover op's hidden agenda. Look for telltale signs of discomfort. Signs include overreactions, embarrassment, blushing, stuttering and nervous mannerisms.

Underachievers

3

Office underachievers come in every age, educational background and ethnic group. They can be male or female, shy or outgoing, charming or hostile, smart or stupid. But they all have one thing in common—they're not living up to the potential that you, as an executive and often their manager, are sure they possess.

It's often unclear with underachievers exactly what the problem is. They may be suffering from learning disabilities, personal problems, a poor educational background or poor work habits. Or they may be doing a bad job because they're ill-suited or unmotivated to do the particular job they've been assigned. In most cases, underachievement is due more to attitude than to lack of ability.

In order to have an effect on someone's attitude, a manager has to go beyond stereotypes. It is nonproductive to simply label an employee incompetent, lazy or no good. Each underachiever is an individual. In your approach, be sensitive to his particular problem.

A turnaround tale

Susan, the manager of public relations for a large Midwestern advertising company, has had a few remarkable successes turning around underachieving employees. One example was Amanda, who had a bad attitude and a giant-size chip on her shoulder. Amanda didn't say hello to anyone, and she was surly and uncooperative. There was obviously something bothering her, but no one could get it out of her. Other employees were complaining about how hard it was to work with Amanda. Things had deteriorated to the point where the next step was to fire her.

Susan's first action was to compose a warning memo to Amanda about general productivity. That spurred a break in Amanda's refusal to communicate. She got angry and wanted to talk. Susan and Amanda had a private conference, and the truth started to come out. Amanda felt that she was being discriminated against because she was black. She'd been transferred to Susan's department because her former manager did not know how to motivate her. He was afraid that, whatever approach he took, he would be accused of racial discrimination. So Amanda had started off in her new position under a cloud, and her attitude made it worse.

Susan said, "I found out from talking to her that she had a lot of ambition. She genuinely wanted to do a good job and get ahead. People saw her as rude and uncooperative, but Amanda thought they were being abusive. My approach with her was, 'What can we do to make you more productive?' First, I asked what she thought. Then, I came up with some suggestions and invited her to choose among them. I told her I expected her to be a productive member of the department team, which meant not having the attitude of 'What can you do for me?' but rather 'What can I do for the company?' I explained that the second attitude is how you get promotions and acknowledgment. I asked her what she needed to turn the situation around. In addition to her people and attitude problems, Amanda didn't understand exactly what was expected of her on the job."

Instead of punishing Amanda for her underachievement, Susan did the opposite. "I gave her an account to be responsible for, and I taught her two or three advanced account management programs on the computer. This boosted her self-image and made her feel like a real member of the department team, on equal standing with everyone else. My basic technique was to give her a lot of training and self-esteem boosting.

"I was also more friendly. When there was a problem, I asked her to talk about it, which opened the channels of communication. I'd even discuss personal things, like family and children, with her. I also asked the people in my department to give her another chance, which they did.

"It was amazing. Everyone saw the chip on her shoulder melt away. Now, Amanda has a new wardrobe, works late and has pride in herself and her work. Two to three months after her turnaround, I proposed giving her a bonus and a raise. Amanda is now one of the most valuable people we have."

Dealing with underachievers requires using your judgment and knowledge of human psychology. Not everyone can be turned around. Some people will have to be let go. But expecting more from underachievers and boosting their self-esteem are crucial. Remember that underachievers come in all shapes and sizes. Don't assume that, because of their sex or race, a particular employee is destined to be an underachiever.

- **Put yourself in the underachiever's place** and ask yourself, "How would this affect me?" This will give you somewhere to start when you sit down to talk. *Example:* Susan put herself in Amanda's place and asked herself, "How would I feel as a woman of color in a clerical position in an all-white department of mostly higher titles?" When she sat down with Amanda, she opened the conversation with, "I can understand that you might feel uncomfortable here. How can we change our behavior to help you fit in?"

- *Talk about it.* Communication is the key to managing anyone—underachievers and everyone else. If you can't seem to communicate with the underachiever, get one of the person's peers to sit in on the meeting. Maybe the peer can get through where you can't.

- *Expect more from them.* What you expect from people is often what you get. If you write off an underachiever, he is likely to live up to your low expectations. Underachievers need *more,* not less, responsibility.

- *Boost their self-esteem.* Many underachievers desperately need to be told how well they're doing, and they must be given acknowledgment and support. They especially need you to acknowledge their intelligence and professionalism.

- *Keep them stimulated* and try to help them grow. *Example:* Assess people's competence who are low on the totem pole and then give them tutorial programs. This approach has a twofold benefit: (1) If they're learning more, they'll feel better about themselves. (2) If they feel better about themselves, the company will benefit. *Example:* Susan assigns lower-level word processors the tutorial programs that come with advanced software computer programs. This increases their reading skills as well. The tutorial programs overexplain, forcing workers to learn a lot.

- *Use cross-training,* i.e., train people to train. Using lower-level workers to train others serves as a morale booster. Plus, when they train, they learn more themselves. Underachievers who are stimulated have a better attitude, their productivity is higher and they have more self-esteem.

- *Use the team approach.* This is often a successful approach with underachievers. You want to draw them into a unit that's bigger than they are and give them a purpose outside themselves. They need to know that their emotional connection with the company has a direct effect on company profits. If they don't care what happens to the company, they're out the door. They have to feel pride in their work and pride in their team membership.

- *Don't be afraid to discipline underachievers.* Employees, especially underachievers, need a bit of discipline and structure. They need to know that someone's watching. Not everyone can function independently. Instead of making the manager the disciplinarian, try to set it up so the team acts as the disciplinary influence.

Coasters

The coaster is the underachiever who is looking for a free ride. Coasters are people of any age or background who want to do as little as possible for their paycheck. He comes in late, takes a long lunch, leaves early and has a laissez-faire attitude toward the job. To a coaster, if the work gets done, fine—if not, that's OK, too. The coaster has little or no company loyalty; he's primarily interested in looking out for No. 1.

Despite their self-centeredness, coasters can be very pleasant personally, and they aren't easily upset. Even if you get angry with them, you usually don't get much of a reaction. Coasters' one positive feature is that they tend to be easygoing—probably because they don't take work (or life) too seriously.

The coaster is genuinely bewildered when you show concern about doing things the right way. He thinks you're too picky and exacting. The coaster can't fathom why little things are so important to you, like spelling customers' names correctly, meeting deadlines or keeping track of inventory.

We're all forced to to deal with telephone operators who can't spell, bank tellers who can't add, customer service representatives who aren't any help and sales clerks who don't know anything about what they're selling. No company is free of this kind of employee because they all have to hire workers, and it's difficult to hire in a tight labor market.

Some high school and college graduates are used to getting by with mediocre work or worse. When they are out in the working world, it comes as a shock that their boss wants more from them than they produced in school. This doesn't mean that all coasters are lazy by nature. Some actually want to do good work, but they simply don't have the background. Once they see how limited they are, they are discouraged and start coasting. Not only do they have to be motivated, but they have to be trained and educated. You can't simply fire them because you're unlikely to find anyone better at their level. Spend time with them. Determine what engages them, what might motivate them to do better work. Factor that information into how you assign their duties.

Observation: Some coasters do have the intelligence and skills to do a good job, but are coasting for other reasons. If properly handled and motivated, they can perform well. (See Lifers.)

The following suggestions may help you get satisfactory work from coasters:

- **Give clear assignments.** You may think you give clear assignments, but it's possible that the coaster doesn't totally understand what you expect. You may be overestimating her level of comprehension. Many people today are used to getting information in short sound or visual bites. Explanations and instructions should be broken down into small segments. Convey not only what you want, but also how you want it done. Time factors, priorities and margins for error should also be spelled out.

- **Find out how he feels about the assignment.** You may be starting with the assumption that the coaster will have no trouble doing what you want. But you may be wrong. As you explain the job, observe him carefully. If you see even the smallest sign of lack of enthusiasm, or if he expresses some hesitation, explore further. Ask what problems he anticipates and how he plans to accomplish the task. His responses should tell you what his reservations are.

Caution: Managers often project their feelings onto employees. You feel confident about getting the job done, and you expect your employees to feel the same way. By projecting your feelings onto your employees, you overlook their doubts.

- **Negotiate realistic timetables.** The key word here is "negotiate." What you think of as realistic may not be realistic to the coaster. He may have an entirely different perception of how long it should take to do things. Discuss and agree on specific priorities and schedules.

- **Be specific about dates.** Vague deadlines create misunderstanding. If you can, build a little leeway into the schedule. But once you agree on the deadline, let the coaster know that you expect it to be met.

- **Give appropriate feedback.** Sometimes, poor work comes from management neglect. Some employees feel that no one notices or appreciates their work. *Consider:* Does the employee have enough contact with you? Do you offer rewards, incentives and praise for a job well done? *Important:* Once things are going well, continue demonstrating your support, interest and appreciation.

- **Provide extra help if necessary.** If, after doing all the above, the coaster still doesn't turn in a satisfactory performance, consider other options. If she needs to upgrade her knowledge or skills, provide some training or coaching. If she's coasting even though you're convinced she can do the job, make it clear that she has to measure up. If she fails to do so, she risks termination.

Observation: All coasters require motivation. Give them a lot of support, encouragement and reassurance while you're trying to turn them around.

Lifers

The lifer is usually an older person who has gone as far as he can go in the company; he's become unpromotable. Each lifer has a story. At one point in his career, he was a bright, shining star with a promising future. But then, something happened. Somewhere along the line, he fell into a rut and wound up in his current position, a cubicle in the far reaches of the company's least-accessible floor. Now, he just wants to get out of the organization with his pension intact. He'll be the first to go for early retirement if it's offered.

Lifers don't want to do much, but they're not out to get anyone, either. They can be very nice people. Unless the company falls on hard times or is merged with another firm, management often keeps lifers on because they have no good reason to get rid of them. They do their work competently, if unimaginatively, and they are content with the smallest of raises every few years. (*Note:* If the trend toward downsizing continues, this problem may not be one you encounter as frequently in the years ahead.)

Some executives hate to manage lifers because they see them as deadwood—drains on the department's budget—who do very little for their salaries. And, by virtue of seniority, those salaries may be quite large.

However, if an executive is willing to manage imaginatively, lifers can literally be brought back to life.

Lifers are usually fearful people from family backgrounds where they were overprotected and isolated. Their parents constantly warned them about the dangers of participating fully in the outside world. They learned early that taking risks was foolish and could even lead to disaster.

Managers often make the mistake of writing off lifers. They're ignored and given only the simplest, most menial tasks. But this can be a mistake. They have a wealth of experience that can be used advantageously. They've usually been with the company longer than anyone else, and they know where the information—and the bodies—are buried.

Although the lifer may look like he long ago died and went to heaven, when questioned about the company's procedures and policies, his answers are often clear and perceptive. He knows very well what's going on and why; he just has no inclination to do anything about it. You may even be able to get a lifer to solve a problem that top management had planned to hire a high-priced consultant to deal with.

One of the things smart business consultants do as soon as they're brought into a firm to remedy a problem is ferret out the lifers who've been kicked upstairs. They take them out to lunch and pump them for information. (Of course, not-so-smart consultants try to figure things out on their own, often with disastrous results.) *Example:* A large manufacturing company called in a consulting firm to overhaul its payroll systems. The consultant ignored good old Fred in personnel, who had long ago blended in with the wallpaper, but who'd been handling a crucial aspect of payroll for the last 30 years. The system was organic, built up little by little as the company expanded. By ignoring Fred, the consulting firm created a program so filled with glitches that it took an additional year to fix it.

The ambitious young executive who just took over a department generally has nothing but contempt for lifers. He can't understand how anyone could be content with so little for so long. As a result, he will treat the lifer like part of the furniture. The lifer will respond in kind, doing even less than usual. The lifer doesn't want to be talked down to by a young upstart who doesn't know anything about the company. The executive can't understand why this guy gets paid for just taking up space—why he can't be replaced with someone young and ambitious and hardworking. A lot of resentment builds up in both directions.

But the lifer is only a difficult employee if he is treated like one. When treated with the respect due his years and experience, he can be extremely valuable. He will have an enormous fund of knowledge about company history that can be very helpful to an executive who is feeling his way around for the best methods to handle various problems.

- *Get the lifer on your side.* Lifers are used to being written off, so don't fall into that trap. Try giving a lifer a challenging assignment, but with a lot of discreet support. He may not have done anything difficult in many years, and he may be somewhat rusty. With the proper supervision, however, you may revive his dormant talents and skills. Once you instill some self-confidence into the lifer, you will

have a capable staffer as well as a loyal, grateful employee.

- *Don't give the lifer a high-pressure assignment.* The one thing that will make him fall apart is a great deal of stress. In times of crisis, lifers are sometimes promoted to positions of authority within a company. That's the kiss of death for them, sometimes literally. Lifers aren't geared to handle crisis pressures, and they may get either physically or emotionally sick as a result.

Peddlers

The peddler badgers everyone in the office to buy this or that product, join a pyramid scheme, sign up for get-rich-quick workshops or buy raffle tickets. There are some peddlers who do their work discreetly, in the lunchroom or during coffee breaks. Others burst into your office at the worst possible moment, interrupt phone calls or other important business and won't take no for an answer. And they don't just harass you; they go after your secretary and other staffers as well. Just when you're about to go into someone's office to discuss business, there's the peddler taking up the person's spare chair.

Peddlers are like buzzing flies. They don't do any real harm, but they're so annoying that you can't get any work done when they're around. When you try to swat them by saying something like "I'm busy now," they're unfailingly friendly and chirp back, "I'm so sorry to bother you, I'll come back later." You want to snap, "Don't bother," but you don't want to insult this good-natured person who is only trying to raise a few bucks, after all.

Everyone knows that company life can get pretty boring. Peddlers make life more interesting by giving people something to look forward to. The anticipation of a new lotion, jewelry or cookies arriving, or winning a new car in a raffle, provides a break from the daily routine. Moreover, peddlers seem to be such a minor annoyance that you tend to put up with them. After all, who wants to be labeled a bad sport?

No one wants to be the Scrooge who didn't allow his staff to buy Girl Scout cookies or contribute to a worthy cause. And that's where the peddler's leverage comes in. You can't get rid of one without looking like a bad guy.

There is a way to handle peddlers in the office. Don't totally banish them because you'll engender staff resentment. Instead, make sure they do their selling on your terms, not theirs:

- *Limit their activities.* There's no reason that peddlers should be allowed to sell their wares anytime they please. They can be limited to lunch hour in the lunchroom, coffee breaks or before or after work. If you want to be a little more liberal, allow peddling for a half-hour at the end of the day, when staffers are less likely to be busy.
- *Monitor what they are selling.* It might be illegal without the seller even knowing it. *Example:* pyramid schemes. Some that came under fire from attorneys general all over the country were all the rage in offices. If you suspect there's something fishy going on in your office, call your local department of consumer affairs or state attorney general's office.
- *Provide other positive distractions to alleviate office boredom.* Staffers shouldn't have to waste money to have something fun to anticipate. *Suggestions:* Exercise programs, workshops, seminars and social get-togethers.
- *Co-opt the peddlers* by providing items to buy through the company. *Suggestion:* There are book distribution services that bring stacks of the latest best-sellers—plus how-to and self-help books—to offices and factories and arrange for them to be sold in the lunchroom or lounge. If you provide books for sale, at least you'll be encouraging reading instead of junk food consumption or gambling.

Space Cadets

We all know this rather endearing type. She is still living in the Seventies; she often comes to work looking like she straggled in from an Eagles concert. The space cadet is a friendly, nice person who never argues or talks back, but she seems to be living on a different planet. Let's call the space cadet in this example John.

In one possible scenario, you tell John, "Please make sure Mr. Connor gets the Smithers report by next Tuesday." John replies, "Is that Mr. Connor from Terrazo Corp?" Because you've never heard of Terrazo Corp. but you—and John—have been working for years with Mr. Connor from Jamestown Supplies, your bewildered reply is, "I don't know any Mr. Connor from Terrazo Corp."

John replies, "But a Mr. Connor from Terrazo Corp. called last week about a report."

At this point, you start getting worried. Maybe this call from Mr. Connor from Terrazo Corp. was important. You innocently ask John, "Why didn't you tell me

a Mr. Connor from Terrazo Corp. called?" John replies, "Because you'd just talked to him." "But that was Mr. Connor from Jamestown," you snap back, your under-the-collar area heating up.

"How was I to know there was another Mr. Connor?" John replies, looking hurt.

"Because you've been talking to him for years, you idiot!!" you want to reply, but don't. You wouldn't want to hurt poor John's feelings. In the past, he has actually been known to cry when you hurt his feelings, which made your stomach churn with embarrassment. Instead, you grit your teeth and frantically try to locate the other Mr. Connor. John meanwhile has totally forgotten about the report, which the first Mr. Connor will probably never get—unless you remember it and remind John one more time.

Why, you may ask, would anyone keep John on staff? There are many reasons. He may be the boss' son-in-law who can't get a job anywhere else. Or your company may have very strict rules on firing. Or John may not be in your department, but you still have to deal with him on a regular basis.

Or you may be John's enabler. John, after all, is probably a very sweet fellow who notices when you look down and asks about your emotional and physical health. You've had a few beers with him and reminisced about the '86 Mets. His wife has left him, and he's trying to support three kids on his own. You know that if you fire John, he'll lose his house and wind up on welfare, and you can't bear to be responsible for that.

Offices, like families, have some smart members, some charming members and some who are, to put it charitably, a bit different. In the office, as in the family, space cadets can be a positive addition to a well-rounded staff if they are handled correctly.

- *Accept him as he is.* Space cadets will never be eager beavers or self-motivators. But that very lack is an asset. Space cadets can be loyal, trustworthy employees who won't try to undermine you or take your job. If treated well, they'll stay with the firm forever and be content with a modest salary. If you accept that your space cadet has limits, and you work within those limits, your professional relationship can be gratifying.
- *Don't trust his judgment.* Many employees can use their judgment to make decisions about what is or isn't important, or what does or doesn't need to be done. Space cadets can't. You have to explain what is required, in detail and preferably in writing. *Example:* John should have been told to report

all phone calls, whether or not he thought his boss already knew about them. John's boss should give him all of his assignments in writing. He should also insist that John write all assignments on his calendar immediately after they are given.

- *Offer practical help.* Pay attention to your space cadet's specific weakness and send him to a seminar that offers to remedy the problem. Or order a self-help book, and follow up on the result. Most space cadets have problems with organization. Workshops on improving organization skills are common, and there are also a number of good books available on the subject.
- *Don't enable.* Realize that you, as a manager, don't have the arbitrary right to excuse people from working. Teamwork means following team rules. If your space cadet is really not doing his job, make it clear that you understand he has personal problems. Point out to him, however, that you have to run the office. Be understanding but firm. Insist that he shape up, and offer whatever support you can.
- *Find out what your space cadet is really good at.* Many space cadets are artistic or creative. Try to make use of their unused talents. You might wind up with a beautifully designed booth for a trade fair, a creative company logo or a well-written brochure for much less than it would cost to send the job out to a professional.

Success-Phobes

Some difficult people are as much a problem to themselves as to others. Just when they're about to get that raise or promotion, they trip themselves up. They fail to hand in a crucial report, have an attack of sulkiness, get drunk on the job or act extremely pushy and obnoxious.

Success-phobes are frustrating to manage because they have such enormous potential. Many people find it hard to overlook potential. Every day, we see people who obviously could do much better than they're doing. We often think it would be a simple matter for them to snap out of whatever problem they're having. Usually, it's not that simple.

It is easy, however, to get trapped into helping a success-phobe. They're often highly intelligent, charming and extremely talented people, which is how they accomplished so much despite their fear of success. You're lured into thinking they just need some good, solid advice to start down the right track. So you try to help them, and they say, "Yes, but...."

You make a suggestion. The success-phobe seems to agree, but then she comes up with a totally convincing reason why your suggestion won't work. *Example:* You suggest to someone who's always late that she get up earlier so she won't be at the mercy of traffic jams. She replies, "That's a good idea, but if I get up earlier I'll wake my husband, and he'll be furious at me." You stand there dumbfounded trying to think of a way out of that one.

You may wonder how success-phobes got that way. A common unconscious motive for people who fear success is protecting the feelings of a parent who was a failure by refusing to succeed themselves. Success in the adult world can also be frightening to people who unconsciously fear separating from their parents. To them, being a responsible adult means they won't get taken care of anymore.

Many success-phobes from the baby-boom generation have resisted adult responsibilities because they really don't want to grow up. They want to remain children so they can be protected by others. They're eternal rebels who don't see why they have to adhere to the rules of society. If you happen to supervise such a person, you can be trapped into the role of parent/caretaker.

One of the first steps you must take is to stop being an office enabler. In the world of 12-step-programs such as Alcoholics Anonymous, the term "enabler" is used to describe people who enable the alcoholic or drug addict to continue his addiction. Under the guise of "helping" the addict, the enabler actually makes it easier for him to continue being addicted.

It's easy to become an office enabler to success-phobes. You make allowances for their failures. You know how talented they are and how well they could do if they just applied themselves. Instead of demanding good work, you're indulgent. You put up with a mediocre or unsatisfactory performance because occasionally you get flashes of brilliance from them. You delude yourself into thinking that, if you're understanding and encouraging enough, the success-phobes will live up to their potential. Somehow, that never happens.

You have to start putting your foot down with success-phobes. As long as they have supervisors and co-workers who put up with them, they'll stay stuck. To change their behavior, you have to stop feeding into it. Here's how:
- *Expect more, not less,* from the success-phobe. This person is very capable. As long as you're willing to take less, that's what you'll get.

- *Give out big assignments in small increments.* Sometimes, an entire project with a long deadline is too threatening to a success-phobe. She may be better able to do it one small piece at a time.
- *Give constructive support.* If the success-phobe is struggling with a project, don't allow her to hand it in late or unfinished. Instead, offer practical help. Maybe the success-phobe could use a researcher, or someone to make phone calls, or someone to give technical assistance.
- *Suggest therapy.* It's enormously helpful to people with a fear of success to understand the unconscious motives for their problem.

Substance Abusers

Substance abuse has become a serious threat to American business. Identifying and eliminating employees under the influence of drugs and alcohol is a priority to prevent legal problems, accidents and the spread of substance abuse throughout your office.

The abuse of illegal drugs has very real costs to your company and may be more pervasive than you think. The U.S. Chamber of Commerce estimates that drug and alcohol abuse costs employers $160 billion a year and affects as much as 23 percent of the work force. The Chamber also warns that employees who use drugs:

- Are one-third less productive and incur 300 percent higher medical costs than employees who don't use drugs.
- Are late three times more often; request early dismissal or time off twice as often.
- Use three times more sick benefits.
- Are five times more likely to file workers' compensation claims.
- Often sell drugs to other employees, or steal from co-workers to support their habits.

What can't be measured are the costs companies incur through diminished quality, disrupted relationships and impaired judgment. People under the influence of illegal drugs simply can't perform to the best of their ability.

Alcoholism may be even more devastating to companies than addiction to illegal drugs because it's more common. It's also more insidious because drinking is legally and socially acceptable. There's a higher level of denial when it comes to interpreting alcohol use as alcohol abuse. Many alcoholics feel that as long as they show up for work every day, they don't really have a problem. Getting them to acknowledge that they have no control over their drinking is the most difficult part.

Signs of trouble

An employee who uses drugs may not be an addict. Addiction refers to loss of control, an irresistible compulsion to abuse a substance in increasing doses and with increasing frequency. An employee doesn't have to be addicted to have a substance abuse problem. In this case, a problem is identified as a decline in work performance. You don't even need evidence of substance abuse to address the problem head on.

Nevertheless, if an employee is coming to work late, looks tired a lot, calls in sick regularly, and doesn't do the caliber of work he used to, there's a good chance the reason is drugs or alcohol. Robert Smith of Inter-Care, a New York City outpatient treatment program, says a steady decline from former high job performance is a red flag that something's going on. Another sign of trouble is a feeling of discomfort when working with the individual. If someone's on drugs or abusing alcohol, you often "know" before you know.

It can be difficult to spot a substance-abusing employee when he isn't under the influence. But the symptoms of active use are hard to miss:

- *Signs of alcohol abuse:* Red, mottled facial skin … breath odor… clothes in disarray… slurred speech… inappropriately friendly or hostile behavior… loss of train of thought… overly cautious movements.
- *Signs of cocaine abuse:* Chronic runny nose and nosebleeds… visits to the restroom resulting in a change to a more lively mood… too talkative or incoherent… speech and movement seem speeded up… has paranoid fantasies.
- *Signs of heroin abuse:* Weight loss and muscle wasting… sleepy eyes, with contracted pupils resembling pinpoints… puncture marks on the arms or other parts of the body… a dreamy, off-in-space look… sleeping on the job… addiction to sweets… extremely jittery (when a fix is needed).
- *Other signs of active alcohol or drug use:* Personality change… unusually violent or passive behavior… glazed eyes… abrasions, bumps or bruises… lingering colds and flu… apparent poor nutrition… slowed reflexes and loss of coordination… inability to concentrate… dizziness or tremors… memory loss or blackouts.

- **Work-related symptoms to watch for:** Inattention or forgetfulness... erratic work quality and production... mood shifts... tardiness or absenteeism... clandestine discussions with non-employees or employees the worker has no reason to be talking to... sudden suspiciousness or secretiveness... legal problems that require time off.

Obviously, you can't diagnose an employee as having a substance abuse problem. You're wise not to because any number of problems, including marital difficulties, a child's illness or a bout of depression, can cause symptoms that appear much like those described above. Accusing someone of drug or alcohol abuse is not only unwise, it could land you in court. Concentrate on work productivity and the employee's behavior and work quality. Intervene only when those problems begin to get out of hand.

Many managers who suspect substance abuse sidestep the issue because they don't want to deal with an employee who is dependent on drugs or alcohol. Failing to confront declining performance not only perpetuates the problem, but also can enable the employee's substance abuse by allowing the worker to indulge his addiction without consequences. Don't be an enabler.

Substance abusers can also be very manipulative and convincing in getting others to help them. If you feel as though you're being taken for a ride by an employee whose work has been deteriorating lately, you may be dealing with a substance abuser.

How to help

Observe changes in employee behavior. Keep track of changes in productivity and work quality that may suggest an employee has a personal problem that's affecting his work. You need to know your employees well enough to be able to spot variances in behavior that fall outside what you'd normally expect.

- **Document problems in performance.** Absenteeism, tardiness, poor performance and interpersonal conflicts should all be noted in an employee log. Indicate specific names, dates, and times, the nature of the problem and corroborative observations. Keep your records unbiased and secure from other employees.
- **Confront the employee.** Hold an initial meeting with the employee to advise him that his performance is unsatisfactory and that he must make improvements or face disciplinary action. Do not discuss substance abuse—the issue is not what's causing the work problems, but the need to correct them. A separate meeting may be held with the employee's immediate supervisor and the personnel department to establish the nature of the problem and document the disciplinary course.
- **Refer the employee to a professional for assistance with personal problems.** If the employee admits or alludes to a problem with drugs or alcohol, recommend that he seek professional help. If your company has an employee assistance program, it can provide a referral. If your firm doesn't have such a program, you can contract with an outside organization to provide this kind of service. Otherwise, suggest the employee see his physician. Don't get involved in diagnosing the employee's problem or evaluating treatment options. Keep the discussion focused solely on performance issues.
- **Follow up on the employee's performance.** Continue maintaining detailed, objective records of the employee's performance. If there is no improvement, begin disciplinary action as you would for any other performance problem.

Substance abuse and the law

Congress drafted the ADA broadly to provide disabled Americans the opportunity for gainful employment. Congress recognized that some disabilities, by their nature, are special and pose safety risks. Drug and alcohol addiction are two such disabilities.

The ADA requires employers to walk a fine line between enforcing reasonable workplace safety and behavioral rules and making accommodations for those who are addicted to drugs or alcohol.

As a general rule, employers are allowed to enforce reasonable workplace rules against coming to work under the influence and against disruptive behavior, even if that behavior may be associated with an addiction to drugs or alcohol. That is, employers can punish inappropriate behavior and require that employees show up clean and sober.

The waters become murkier, however, when workers addicted to drugs or alcohol want to clean up their act. In some circumstances, you may be required to accommodate their attempts. In addition, they may be eligible for leave under the Family and Medical Leave Act. Under the ADA, what the employee is addicted to makes a difference in how much leeway you must provide as an employer.

The ADA does not protect current users of illegal (i.e., "street") drugs. It does, however, protect those who've shaken their addiction sufficiently to no longer be classified as active illegal drug users. You should offer these workers reasonable accommodations to keep them on track: for example, time off for therapy, counseling and attending Narcotics Anonymous meetings or even inpatient care for related psychiatric problems like depression.

You can fire current drug users even if their work isn't suffering. Just be sure that the use in question is really "current." The ADA specifies that a worker who is "currently engaged in the illegal use of drugs" isn't covered by the law. The EEOC has taken the position that "current" means "the illegal use of drugs that has occurred recently enough to indicate that the individual is actively engaged in such conduct."

The EEOC's Technical Assistance Manual provides that "current drug use means that the illegal use of drugs occurred recently enough to justify an employer's reasonable belief that involvement with drugs is an ongoing problem. It is not limited to the day of use, or recent weeks or days, in terms of an employment action. It is determined on a case-by-case basis."

So how long does it have to have been since the worker took drugs before the ADA protects him? What if your drug tests take three weeks to come back from the lab? Can he argue that any action you take against him three weeks later violates the ADA because he's now a "former" drug user? The answer is unclear. Your best bet is to make sure that any action you take against him is based on his violation of an established workplace rule, not just the fact that he had a positive drug test.

The ADA covers workers who are alcoholics even if they currently drink. To be covered by the ADA, alcoholics' addiction must be severe enough to substantially impair a major life function such as taking care of themselves. Many heavy drinkers may meet that test. That doesn't mean, however, that you have to tolerate alcoholics coming to work drunk. Courts have consistently held that employers have the right to establish reasonable workplace rules, including coming to work clean and sober.

Former drug users

To protect yourself from lawsuits by former addicts, follow these guidelines:

- **Set job-related rules** against coming to work under the influence of drugs or alcohol.
- **Establish behavioral rules** such as demanding punctuality and regular attendance, allowing for appropriate FMLA absences.
- **Apply the rules consistently.** That is, if you fire someone who comes to work high, you should terminate those who show up drunk. In both cases, you're punishing behavior (intoxication), not a disability (alcoholism or addiction).
- **Keep records of whom you discipline and why.** Review how you discipline workers who violate your rules with an eye toward identifying patterns. For example, see if you've disciplined those who come to work late because of an addiction more harshly than those who show up late for other reasons such as "traffic" or "car trouble." Remember, a neutral rule created for a valid business purpose, applied evenhandedly, will stand up in court.

Recreational drug use or binge drinking

Not everyone who uses drugs (legal or illegal) or drinks alcohol is disabled. Remember, to be a disability, a condition must substantially limit a major life activity. A worker who sometimes smokes marijuana or a social drinker who sometimes is hung over on Monday is probably not disabled. Neither is covered by the ADA or needs to be accommodated.

In fact, you should enforce all workplace rules against these workers. The reason is simple: If you go easy on weekend drinkers or drug users when you catch them and then land heavily on the true addict, you may create an ADA case. You would, in effect, be applying your neutral policy ("Don't come to work under the influence") to the disadvantage of the disabled addict. Define the crime, and then make sure everyone who breaks the rules does the time.

Wise Guys

The wise guy is the employee who is too smart for his own good. These are the smart alecks who always think they know better than you how to do things, who make inappropriate jokes about higher-ups in the company and who are always testing the rules to see how much they can get away with.

Wise guys can be, and often are, intelligent, capable people who just refuse to take themselves or their work seriously. They're rebels who don't want to conform to the corporate environment. They see themselves as somehow above, or better than, the straightlaced world they're forced to inhabit because they need to pay the rent.

Wise guys call for a two-pronged approach. You need to be assertive with them, or they will take advantage of you. But you also need to give them a lot of support and encouragement to boost their often shaky self-esteem.

Wise guys will take advantage of you unless you keep constant track of them. This doesn't necessarily mean looking over their shoulders, but it does mean being aware of what they're doing. When a wise guy makes a mistake, talk to him about it. When he starts coming in late, have a little chat about lateness being bad for morale. And so on.

Don't get too authoritarian with wise guys. They're rebels who can't resist defying orders. They need a lot of structure and discipline, but they are also willing to listen to reason. *Example:* As summer approached, the wise guy in a small public relations firm took his usual dressed-down look from sportswear casual to outright beachwear—right down to his sandals. The firm had no dress code, but it worked primarily with very conservative business clients. The wise guy's boss called him into her office and tried to get him to look at himself from the outside. Without telling him not to dress that way anymore, she brought up the image the company wanted to project. She asked him how it would look if a client came by and saw him in his present attire. The wise guy just shrugged. But the following day, he had changed back to sportswear.

The wise guy needs a lot of positive reinforcement. Like all underachievers, beneath his rebellious posture is a poor self-image. The rebellious behavior is often a cry for attention, help and support. A wise guy tries to get away with the bare minimum because, at some level, he doesn't feel he can really do any better. He's using his rebellious posture to get off the hook, to lower others' expectations of him.

One effective strategy for dealing with a wise guy is to tell him you expect more of him because you know he's worth more. Tell him he's smarter and capable of doing better than he's doing. And assign him real work with real deadlines and the responsibility for meeting them. But don't pull any punches with him; if he fails to do the work, put him on notice.

Other Difficult Personalities

A ccording to psychiatrist John Oldham, scientists are beginning to find proof that the foundations of personality are inherited. To psychiatrists, the inborn, biological, genetic aspects of personality are called temperament.

Personality is like a deck of cards. We're dealt a hand at conception. Our life experiences determine which genetic cards will turn up. Because our innate traits determine how we react to things, these genetic cards determine what the nature of our experiences will be. Your hand—or personality style—will be fairly set by the end of childhood (about age 12). You will hold that hand (have that personality) for the rest of your life.

We do, of course, grow and change throughout life—but in a characteristic manner that depends on our personalities. Most people have a built-in flexibility that allows them to deal with hurdles in their path. They adapt to change, which makes a variety of experiences possible. Others, however, find themselves up against the same old walls. They're locked into rigid, inflexible personality patterns that cause them to have the same disruptive or unsatisfying experiences throughout life. The personalities we'll explore in this section all share these traits. Even the mercurials are locked in. They are unable to overcome their intense emotionality, and, therefore, they cannot see others realistically.

Many people with difficult personalities do not realize that there is anything wrong with them. They're frequently in conflict with family members, employers, colleagues and subordinates. These problems are difficult to resolve because such people usually don't recognize that their own repetitive patterns of behavior contribute to their troubles.

In this section, we examine a few of the more troublesome personality styles that you're likely to run into at the office. We offer some suggestions on how to deal with them. You can't change these people, but you can live with them.

Observation: Remember that few people fall neatly into one category. When you're putting together a strategy for dealing with a particular person, consider both his primary and secondary personality traits. Center your strategy on developing tactics for dealing with the most dominant—or dangerous—trait, but tailor it to the person's secondary traits and tactics for dealing with them as well.

Mercurials

Mercurials are the really moody types. You never know what to expect from them from one day to the next. One day, they love you and are all smiles. But the next day, they glower at you or blow up at you. Then they ignore you for a while. You go in and out of favor, with no explanation or rationale.

Mercurial behavior is extremely upsetting. Not knowing what to expect from someone you depend on can lead to feelings of disorientation and self-doubt. Any insecurities you already have can be magnified by the mercurial person, and we are all insecure in one way or another.

Not knowing where you stand with a mercurial violates the natural human need for reliable, stable and predictable human relationships. Unpleasant though it may be, most of us would prefer dealing with someone who is consistently hostile rather than with a person who veers from hostility to friendliness to indifference. If you know what to expect, you can relax and develop a coping style that you know is effective. But mercurials are, above all else, inconsistent. What works with them today may not work tomorrow.

To understand mercurials, you have to begin by realizing that they are highly emotional. They experience their feelings more intensely than the rest of us, and so they tend to act in extreme ways. They feel hot fury and ice-cold rage and see the world in black-and-white terms. Although most of us try to hide our feelings, mercurials are emotionally uninhibited.

Their emotions affect their thinking as well. They have strong opinions and state them in no uncertain terms. The problem is that those opinions can vary from day to day depending on their moods. This magnifies the problem: One day you have someone who believes in working as a team; the next day, he thinks his word should be law. But whatever the mercurial's opinions are, they won't be wishy-washy.

Mercurials don't take things lightly, especially when it comes to other people. Relationships are very important to them, and they react strongly to everything other people do. It's easy to affect them—with flattery, with rejection, with anger or affection. In fact, strong emotions create the mercurial personality. People who are more influenced by the head than the heart will tend to think things out and depend on reason rather than quick emotional responses. Mercurials are basically immature in their emotional development. Like self-centered children, they react to the most trivial incidents.

Observation: Being at the mercy of your emotions isn't a whole lot of fun. If you work for or with mercurials, keep in mind that they may be suffering even more than you are.

The mercurial boss

When the boss is a mercurial, "What mood is he in today?" is the perennial question. Depending on the answer, the mood of the whole office may change. If the boss is in a good humor, the atmosphere in the firm becomes lighter and people smile and chat. If the boss's mood is bad, an aura of gloom may descend over the entire company.

According to Dr. Oldham, "The mercurial personality style does not carry with it a gift for leadership because mercurials can't establish the necessary managerial detachment from subordinates. They like to become intensely involved, and they end up idealizing relationships. They expect extraordinary personal dedication and perfect performance from those who work for them. When subordinates don't meet those expectations, mercurial managers feel personally let down. They often split those around them into an in-group and an out-group, although affiliation among the favored few is never guaranteed for long. They haven't much planning ability in money matters or in the organization as a whole."

Being mercurial is not all bad, however. According to Oldham, a bit of the mercurial style, which is intense and emotional, may inspire employees to do their best. Mercurials can, and often do, come up with brilliant ideas. If their seconds-in-command are solid, conscientious and noncompetitive, they may work well together. However, if you're a creative, emotional type yourself and you work for a mercurial, this may be a bad combination.

The biggest problem in dealing with a mercurial boss is how he makes you feel. Very few of us have unshakable self-esteem. How others treat us is a major factor in how we feel about ourselves. When we get approval and friendliness from others, we feel good about ourselves; disapproval and hostility make us feel bad. When someone reacts negatively, it's natural to wonder what you've done to insult or anger him.

When you deal with someone who *consistently* rejects you or shows anger, you eventually realize that the problem is the other person's, not yours. Then you can adjust your reactions to deal with the situation. But with a mercurial personality, you may begin to judge yourself according to how that person treats you from moment to moment. That's because most of us depend on consistent feedback from others to feel secure. If someone as important as a boss is extremely mercurial, the ground may feel like it's shifting beneath our feet. We may begin to have doubts about our competence.

Here are some suggestions for dealing with a mercurial boss:

- *Constantly remind yourself that it's him, not you.* Stand back from the outburst of the moment and remind yourself that you are a competent and worthwhile human being, no matter what your boss happens to think about you today.
- *Cultivate a strong internal sense of self-worth.* Every time a mercurial boss makes you doubt yourself, remind yourself of all the projects you've completed successfully. Remember all the times in the past when she praised you to the skies.
- *Enjoy being on a pedestal while it lasts, but recognize that it won't last.* Prepare yourself emotionally for a fall. The mercurial person idealizes and adores people for a while, showering them with compliments and admiration. Because mercurials see things in extremes, however, the new shining star of the company will eventually make a mistake. Then he will be beneath contempt. For the mercurial personality, there is no middle ground.
- *When you do fall from the pedestal, remind your mercurial boss of reality.* Because he doesn't think of people as fallible humans, but as gods or good-for-nothings, inject a touch of reality by reminding him that everyone makes mistakes. You are, after all, a mere mortal; you cannot produce perfect work at all times. Ask for acceptance and understanding of your human fallibility. This approach tends to help.

Mercurial employees

A mercurial subordinate, just like a mercurial boss, can throw you off kilter with his wide mood swings. If you're expecting enthusiasm and cooperation on a project and the mercurial member of your department mopes and looks miserable, it can dampen your optimism. You may even start doubting your own ability.

Call the moody staffer into your office and ask in a concerned way what the problem is. Mercurial people often expect you to read their minds and understand why they're so unhappy. You may have done something to hurt or insult your mercurial employee, but she will never tell you what it is unless you ask.

Once the problem is out in the open, however, the mercurial employee will feel a lot better and often forget all about it. Mercurial people need a lot of positive feedback in order to function. They need to hear how well they're doing, how special they are, and how much you value their work. If they feel you're on their side and notice how well they're doing, mercurials can be dedicated, valuable employees. They can also be very loyal to a boss who appreciates them.

Caution: If a mercurial employee does do a bad job, the worst thing you can do is blow up at him or be extremely critical. Criticize softly. Cushion the criticism with praise for past accomplishments, and make it clear how he can improve next time.

Zip-Lips

"How do you think it went?" John asked Clem, his boss, as they left the meeting where John had presented his sales strategy for a new product. "Fine," said Clem with a tight-lipped smile. John walked back to his office feeling that, as usual, he had no idea what Clem really thought.

If you have to work closely with uncommunicative people, you know how frustrating or annoying it can be. A zip-lip boss is the worst.

Although we might pretend not to care what others think, we work for approval as much as for a paycheck. Therefore, it takes a supremely self-assured individual to feel confident that he's doing a good job without feedback from above.

The zip-lip isn't necessarily nasty, or unlikable, or a bad person, but his lack of communicativeness drives you crazy. Not only are you in the dark about what the zip-lip thinks of you and your work, but also your boss fails to give you vital information that you need to do a good job.

And there's another problem as well: In addition to the annoyance of never knowing what he's thinking, the zip-lip may turn you into a blabbermouth. Many of us get uncomfortable during long silences and tend to fill up the void with chatter. Sometimes, we find ourselves saying things we wish we hadn't said, and we feel all the more uncomfortable when we don't know how the other person is reacting.

There is no single cause for a zip-lip's behavior. People clam up for a number of reasons. They may simply be timid and shy; they don't talk much because it makes them uncomfortable. Or it may be a cultural difference. Members of certain groups, such as New Englanders, tend to be taciturn. They think keeping your thoughts to yourself is a sign of politeness and that people who talk too much are rude. They only talk when they have something to say. And when they do talk, what they say is often understated.

Other zip-lips are sadists who want to see you squirm. Withholding information or approval is their way of controlling others and meting out punishment. For still others, silence is a way to avoid telling a blunt truth. Instead of saying something hurtful or provocative, the zip-lip calculates that it's better to say nothing. Or the zip-lip may simply be avoiding something he doesn't want to acknowledge about himself or you.

Don't focus on how insecure the zip-lip makes you feel. This will give you a false reading about her because you'll be projecting your own feelings onto the situation. For example, you may be feeling that your zip-lip boss isn't saying anything about your report because she doesn't like it. But for all you know, she may be jealous that you did such a good job.

Here are some ways to figure out what you're dealing with:

- *Watch how the zip-lip deals with others.* Question co-workers about her. Is it just you who gets the silent treatment? Or is she this way with everyone? In what situations is the person most silent?
- *Look at the zip-lip's actions.* Is the zip-lip a person who shows respect for you in other ways? If she's your boss, does she give you important assignments and regular raises? Or does the zip-lip seem to have a grudge against you? If you're perceptive, actions may reveal more to you than words.
- *Is the zip-lip withholding valuable information from you, or just his approval?* If information is the issue, there may be another reason for the silent treatment. *Possibility:* You haven't given the person sufficient recognition and appreciation for his knowledge. Once you show some respect, the zip-lip may give you what you want.

Unzipping the zip-lip

It is possible to get zip-lips to open up if you use the right strategies. Psychologist Robert Bramson suggests the following tactics:

- *Ask open-ended questions.* Ending statements with questions like, "Shall I go on?" or "Do you have anything to add?" won't work with a zip-lip because they can be answered with a yes or no. You want to ask questions that call for an in-depth answer, such as, "What's your reaction so far?" or, "What do you think I can do to improve this proposal?"
- *Use the friendly, silent stare.* Open-ended questions are particularly effective when accompanied by a friendly, silent stare. This calls for a quizzical, expectant expression (eyebrows raised, eyes wide open) and a slight smile. Silence provides a quiet time for both of you to collect your thoughts, and it gives you the same kind of leverage that zip-lips use. Don't get uneasy and fill up the space by returning to the substance of your conversation. This will get the zip-lip off the hook, but it won't help you.
- *Comment on what's happening.* If the silence starts becoming a contest, and you start feeling uneasy, comment on the crazy goings-on. *Good statement:* "I expected you to say something, and you haven't. What does that mean?"
- *Help break the tension.* Here are some questions and statements to help the other person start to talk: "Can you talk about why it's so difficult to say what you're thinking? Are you concerned about my reaction? How do you think I'll react?" "You look distressed. Am I wrong that you're feeling uncomfortable (or annoyed, irritated, impatient)?" *Sample follow-up question:* "If you're not annoyed (or uncomfortable or worried about my reaction), then what were your reasons for not letting me know that your division was no longer handling customer complaints?"
- *If you come up against an "I don't know," this is what to do:* Treat it as a nonresponse, and comment on the fact that your meeting seems to be at an impasse. Then return to your friendly, silent stare. Or reply, "Well, just speculate," and again stay in your expectant stance. Either approach gives you something to say to decrease your own tension and leaves the zip-lip with the ball.

Perfectionists

Perfectionists in the workplace are easy to identify because they procrastinate and tend to waste a lot of time. They put things off; they can't make decisions; they rush to meet deadlines; they're always late; they get stuck on one part of a project. *Example:* They can't get beyond the first paragraph of a report. Instead of coming back to that paragraph, they write it over and over.

The worst office perfectionists are managers who want to make the perfect decision. They never stop gathering data. They never get to the point of actually making the decision because they're so afraid of making the *wrong* decision. *Example:* Adele was in charge of purchasing office copying machines, but she couldn't bring herself to actually buy any copiers. Instead, she constantly did surveys and tried out different brands. She'd lease different models every three months and ask people to rate them. Her office was always short of copiers because Adele couldn't make up her mind.

Some perfectionists won't share their work until it's completely done. If they're involved in some kind of team project, they drive the team crazy because they won't show their work in progress. Other perfectionists tell you too much. They're afraid of leaving anything out, so they snow you under with facts and figures. It's up to you to sort them out.

A lot of perfectionists are at the managerial level because perfectionism often gets people ahead early in their careers. It may make them crazy and give them ulcers, but the drive to do the job right gets them at least to middle management. Then, they project their perfectionism onto others. The perfectionist executive will want everything her secretary types to be absolutely perfect. Or she won't give her secretary enough to do because she's doing it all herself. Why? Because she doesn't trust her secretary. Perfectionists tend to hold on to projects because they don't trust others to do them as well as they want them done.

Perfectionists function fairly well most of the time. They just don't lead balanced lives, and they do things that are counterproductive. But when perfectionists cross the line into real pathology, they become obsessive-compulsives. Obsessive-compulsives are driven perfectionists. They need to be perfect to such an extent that they can't complete anything. And they become so preoccupied with details that they lose sight of what they're doing.

According to Susan Meltsner, M.S.W. and co-author of *The Perfectionist's Predicament* (William Morrow), perfectionists are the easiest type of neurotic to deal with. They're amenable to change because they want to be perfect. They want to be good; they don't want to screw up. As long as they're not full-fledged obsessive-compulsives, they can learn. If you teach them what you want them to do and how you want them to do it—and break it down into small pieces—perfectionists will try their hardest to learn. To change a perfectionist staffer, take an educational approach:

- *Provide structure so that they get things done.* One way to deal with perfectionists is to set interim time deadlines. Make it clear that you want to see part of their work by a certain date. Break tasks down into smaller pieces, and check in with them periodically.
- *If the perfectionist just can't finish something, take the matter out of her hands.* Say, "OK, I will make this decision for you. Now let's talk about what kept you from making the decision."
- *Give a lot of positive feedback.* Perfectionism comes from low self-esteem. Perfectionists are constantly trying to be perfect because they feel so unworthy. They're always insecure about how they're doing, even when they're actually doing very well. If you want to get something from a perfectionist, give him a lot of compliments. The reassurance will bolster him and keep him going.

Perfectionist bosses will criticize everything you do and ask you to do your work over. They may even tell you to do things one way and then, after you're finished, say they really wanted it another way. In order to tolerate this behavior, you have to be secure. You have to be convinced that your work is good, even though you may never hear anyone actually say the words. Here are some ways to deal with perfectionist bosses:

- *Memo everything.* Confirm everything that you're told to do in writing.
- *Check in with your boss regularly.* If he's going to be hovering over your shoulder and checking up on you, check in with him first so you're more in control.
- *Give your boss options.* Tell him how you want to approach a particular project, add a couple of options and ask him to select one. *Purpose:* To lead him in your direction by providing him with the illusion of choice.
- *If all else fails, put your foot down.* Tell your perfectionist boss that there are limits to what you will take. Begin by identifying his intolerably perfectionist demands, then explain the effect they have on you. Define the consequences if the perfectionist doesn't change. *Example:* "When you pick apart my reports, you make me feel as though I'm doing a bad job. I don't think I can continue doing my job well unless I get the sense that you appreciate my work."

Control Freaks

Control freaks border on being obsessive-compulsives. They don't merely have a hands-on attitude; they have a stranglehold on everything their subordinates do. They can't let control out of their hands for a minute. Even when they've supposedly given you a project to do on your own, they're double- and triple-checking to see how it's going.

Control freaks are the ultimate perfectionists. Often, they're workaholics. But they can get bogged down in details and fail to see the big picture. According to Dr. Oldham, "They invest all their energy in work ... but they lose enthusiasm for it. They're tense, strained, anxious and overwhelmed by the amount of work they have to do." However, because they're willing to devote so much time and energy to work, control freaks tend to move up in their professions. They succeed through hard work. They are also loyal and respectful of authority.

Their perfectionist streak, however, may make control freaks indecisive managers. As Dr. Oldham says, "Some need to be so thorough—to check and recheck every detail before coming to any conclusion—that they can be exasperatingly slow to make up their minds, even on minor matters."

Example: Elaine, a 35-year-old marketing executive at a national frozen food company, was working on a campaign for a new product. David, the head of marketing, would not leave her alone. The product had been his idea, and he felt that only he knew how to promote it. A few times a day, he would manage to wander by her office and inquire about the campaign. If she said she was planning to concentrate on print advertising, he'd insist on more TV. If Elaine wanted to push the product for a younger group of consumers, he insisted only older people would want to buy it. He went over every detail of the campaign with her so many times that she thought she would scream. He even explained details that she'd learned on her first job. David simply couldn't let Elaine alone to run the campaign as she saw fit.

Control freaks had parents who were rigid, overbearing and overly critical. As children, pressure was put on them to behave like adults. Many of them were firstborn children who had to take care of younger siblings and didn't have much of a childhood. In order to gain parental approval, they had to overcome their "bad" impulses and feelings. Many control freaks are inwardly very angry, but they can't get outwardly angry because they're so inhibited. They express their anger by being overcontrolling and nitpicking you to death.

People like David nag, check up on you and bombard you with questions and reminders because they're afraid of what would happen if they didn't. They feel that if they let one little detail slip, the whole situation will go out of control—maybe they'd be fired or be blamed for losing the company's biggest client. So they can't let go.

Here are some suggestions for loosening the control freak's grip:

- *Be humorously tolerant.* Let the control freak have his habits. *Example:* If your boss insists on camping out in your office to watch your every move, try asking him if you should have an extra desk and phone line moved in for him.
- *Try passive resistance.* Often the control freak is checking up on so many things at once that if you say, "I'll get back to you on that," he may forget all about it. Try yessing him to death and then going about your own business.
- *Avoid arguments and power struggles.* Control freaks feel they must win—it's their nature. They can back you into a corner with nitpicking arguments until you give in out of exhaustion. Instead of arguing, make a neutral comment like, "I understand what you're saying." Even a control freak can compromise when he realizes you're not out to get him.
- *Don't expect a lot of positive feedback.* You may think your boss doesn't like your work because he never compliments you. But control freaks are very stingy with praise. Inwardly, they may have a very high regard for your work.
- *Detach.* Take a deep breath, and leave the room or hang up the phone. Ignore negative comments. Don't try to get the control freak to agree with you.
- *Admit it when you're wrong.* The control freak will respect you for admitting error.

Bulldozers

Bulldozers are pushy people who are abrasive, insensitive and overly blunt. They ignore the social niceties and say things straight out that others would mention with more circumspection. They're incapable of playing office politics because they have no feeling for the undercurrents in relationships. They have only one behavioral mode—if you want something, keep insisting until you get it.

In the short run, people who are pushy may be very successful. In the long run, however, aggressive people often inadvertently set up hostile relationships with others, so people either actively or passively back away from them.

Observation: A bulldozer is not necessarily a bully. Bullies are power players who sometimes use bulldozing tactics to get what they want. But bulldozers may not be interested in power at all. They just have a personality style that others find difficult to deal with.

Recommendation: Before designating someone a bulldozer, look at your own personality to see if the problem is a matter of personal style. There may simply be a personality clash between two people from very different backgrounds.

Example: Bicoastal culture shock. Jack, a manager at a San Francisco import firm, hired a recently arrived New Yorker, Loretta, as his assistant. He liked Loretta's assertive, can-do style, and he felt she would shake up his overly laid-back department.

She shook it up all right. Within a month, everyone on Jack's staff was furious with her—and at him for hiring her. They were all gossiping behind her back about how pushy she was. Jack, himself a well-brought-up Californian, was very annoyed by some of her behavior, like bursting into his office without knocking, talking so loudly on the phone that the whole office could hear her and demanding what she wanted instead of asking for it politely. But he put up with it because she was a diligent and conscientious worker.

Poor Loretta had no idea what she'd done and didn't understand why everyone soon cut her dead. She went to Jack and asked what was going on. Jack questioned his staffers, and they complained that Loretta was an insensitive bulldozer. They brought up an incident where a supplier had failed to deliver some office equipment by the date promised, including a new chair for Loretta's office. Loretta called up the supplier and made a big stink, speaking to the vice president of the company and complaining about the company's service. The rest of the staff were horrified because they knew and liked the salesperson from that supplier and thought it was extremely rude to get him into trouble. They thought Loretta should have just waited another week or two for the chair to arrive.

This incident started Loretta's bulldozer reputation. What made it worse was that she complained all the time—about the weather, the traffic, the company's health insurance and anything else that struck her wrong.

The problem was a clash of cultural styles. Californians are often much more polite than outspoken New Yorkers, who affect a more aggressive style. In New York, rudeness is a way of life. Complaining is a communal pastime that serves as an emotional safety valve in a city where just getting to work and back home can test your survival skills. In civilized San Francisco, complaining is considered "negativity," a state of mind to be avoided.

Jack, a savvy and sensitive manager, got the whole department together for a luncheon meeting and brought up some of the cultural differences. When Loretta explained, with her sharp sense of humor, what life was like in New York, everyone relaxed and had a good laugh. From then on, her co-workers were more tolerant.

When someone is abrasive, it's hard not to take it personally. You start wondering if it's your fault and what you did to set the person off.

Here's how to deal with bulldozers by shifting the focus away from self-blame:

- *Analyze whether the person just has an abrasive style without any personal intent.* Is it a personality quirk? *Possible underlying reasons:* a family background that encouraged pushiness; a feeling of entitlement, whereby he feels entitled to all the goodies in life; personal problems that make him particularly insensitive.
- *Ask if there is some misunderstanding.* The person may not usually be abrasive. She may just be angry in this situation because she's misunderstood some communication from you. Try to clarify what's going on.
- *Look at yourself.* Are you insecure in certain areas? Is the bulldozer pushing your buttons? Does he remind you of a critical parent or sibling? Are you secretly afraid of being an imposter; are you concerned that he's discovered that you don't know what you're talking about? Once you identify why the bulldozer is getting to you, you'll be able to deal with him much better.
- *Focus on what your goal is with the person.* If your goal is to sell him on the value of a new idea or project, for example, and he responds abrasively or insensitively by putting you down, you have to focus on your goal—to sell that project.
- *Don't focus on "fairness."* When dealing with abrasiveness, a lot of people get hot under the collar because they tell themselves: "He shouldn't be that way; he should be more sensitive; he should understand how important this project is to me." But people sometimes aren't fair; they have their own agendas.
- *Watch for the hidden bargain syndrome.* "I've done good things for this person in the past, therefore I expect him to be fair and compassionate with me." The bulldozer isn't privy to the bargain, and she may have a totally different agenda.

If, after consideration, you decide the person really is a bulldozer, choose a strategy for dealing with the abrasiveness. *Ask yourself:* What's been successful with this person in the past? How defensive is he? Does he blow up easily? Is he able to back off and listen to me?

Dr. Barry Lubetkin suggests using one of these two strategies to deal with bulldozers:

- *Ignore the abrasiveness.* Assume that it has very little to do with you. Frequently, the people who are most upset by pushiness are those who have a history of being unassertive. They feel victimized and overexaggerate their response. This strategy would have been a good one to use with Loretta.
- *Try the minimal effect response.* Then build on it as needed. *First thing to say:* "I understand you're under a lot of pressure, but that remark was really not appreciated." Then escalate slowly in terms of your goal. "Once again, let me repeat, I would like to work with you in a cooperative manner on this project. But if that's impossible, I'll ask that you be assigned to another project."

Don't ever lose your cool, which is what a lot of people tend to do. They go immediately from unassertiveness to total rage, and they end up in a yelling match with the bulldozer. Afterward, they feel bad about losing control of themselves. Because they've managed to humiliate the bulldozer, he probably won't ever do what they want.

Who's the Difficult Person?

Many people you may think are difficult are really just different. Their personalities and behavioral styles may clash with yours. Once you learn to identify others' styles—and honestly assess your own—you can figure out why you're having a problem with a particular type of person.

Four basic styles

Psychologists tell us that there are four basic behavioral styles. Each has positive aspects, which flourish in a supportive, encouraging environment. But paradoxically, it's those very positive aspects that become limitations under stress. Let's take a look at the four basic styles:

- *Extrovert.* This is a person who is open, straight-forward, outgoing and risk-oriented—a gregarious sales type. Extroverts can be very persuasive; but when they overdo it, they become aggressive, pushy, sarcastic and manipulative.
- *Controller.* This is the traditional, bottom-line, results-oriented person who is very direct with people—a top-executive type. When controllers overdo their strengths, they become overly controlling, pushy, demanding, stubborn, rigid and hardheaded.
- *People-pleaser.* This is the peacemaker, harmonizer—a gregarious, approachable, caring type. But people-pleasers can become so interested in the happiness of others that they always give in and always say yes, even when they mean no. The pleasers won't say anything to defend themselves. Instead, they become time bombs—storing negative feelings and carrying them around until, at some point, they blow up. The blowup is usually so unexpected that it's bewildering to the target.
- *Meticulous.* This is an extremely cautious person who is reserved, avoids taking risks and wants things done perfectly. When pushed, meticulous types become avoiders; they avoid tasks and people and fail to get things done.

People with different behavior styles often find it hard to work together. That's the reason why you may be able to work easily with some people, but you find others too intimidating, guilt-provoking or infuriating to deal with. You probably know which type(s) you have trouble with in the following examples:

- People who are controlling often have great problems with people who are emotional and sensitive.
- An extrovert, who's outgoing and doesn't take care of details, often finds it hard to relate to meticulous people. The extrovert may call the meticulous person a difficult person when the latter really isn't difficult—just different. In fact, the meticulous person actually complements the extrovert by taking care of the details the extrovert is likely to overlook.
- An easygoing, people-oriented person will consider the demanding controller difficult because the latter cares more about results than about peoples' feelings. Again, the two are actually complementary personalities. Work teams need both types to get things done.

People-pleasers and meticulous people (and even other extroverts and controllers) often have trouble with extroverts and controllers. When stressed, the controller becomes aggressive and the extrovert becomes sarcastic. Such behavior can make others feel like prey—hardly an asset for team-building.

The solution isn't to get others to change their basic behavioral styles; each style is valuable to the organization. Each type of person is strong in an area where others tend to be weak. The trick is to get the different types to work together so that they make a good team—complementing, not clashing with, one another.

If the workplace is to run smoothly, people-pleasers and meticulous people have to stand up for themselves and confront the sometimes sarcastic and/or abusive behavior of the extroverts and controllers. Extroverts and controllers, in turn, have to control their overbearing behavior and be more sensitive and understanding in their dealings with others.

Are you the difficult person?

Be open to the idea that the difficult person in a given relationship may be you. You may want to change someone at work—most of us do. But people aren't going to change their basic personalities. If you want the situation to change, you're the one who is going to have to change—by learning to work with the other person's personality and behavioral style.

Once, you could control people who worked on an assembly line by standing over them and bossing them all day. But today, nine out of 10 companies are in the information and service business, rather than manufacturing. Says Gilliam, "You can't control people in the service and information business. Many times they're not even physically close to you—they're at a different facility or on a different floor. Sometimes, their job is so technical you may not really understand what they're doing."

Service and information people *can* be managed. But the only way to do that is to support them rather than control them. When you support them, not only do you get better work and more cooperation, but also you use more of their creative potential.

A major hurdle for most executives, says Gilliam, is that they've been trained to see things in terms of getting results. If the results aren't immediately forthcoming, their attitude is, "Get out of my way and let me do it." Often, they don't get the help they want because no one has told the staff what to do or how to do it—or tried to find out what the staff needs to give their best. To make matters worse, staffers who are angry because of the way they're treated by management may do just enough not to be fired. These executives don't realize that the only way to get results is *through* people: If you are sensitive to your staff's needs—including their psychological needs—then they will get the results for you. That's not babying—and it's not turning yourself into some kind of shrink. It's simply recognizing that people aren't nuts and bolts.

Gilliam finds that this is a particularly acute problem for managers who came into the work force as technicians, software designers, engineers and accountants. "They're highly skilled technically," he says, "but they don't know how to deal with people. They're working horrendous hours to get their work done, in part because they're not delegating as much as they could if they had more people skills."

Executives who suffer from low self-esteem may also find themselves constantly at odds with "difficult people." Their own insecurity makes them avoid being assertive managers. The person they call difficult may not be all that bad; he or she is just intimidating because of the executive's own poor self-image.

That's understandable. But executives also have to understand that these people aren't going to stop being assertive just because others don't feel good about themselves. The only way these executives can start feeling better about themselves is to acquire people skills.

"I lead seminars with hundreds of people each year, and no one [in them] has heard of the leading self-help books," Gilliam says. "I'm convinced that's the major problem executives have. If you haven't done anything to improve yourself and you have to deal with people who are learned, well read, say what they think and are assertive, then you're going to be intimidated by those people. It's not their fault; it's your fault because you haven't kept up."

As we said in the introduction to this Report, we're all growing. We need to keep developing ourselves to deal effectively with others. When you start putting into practice some of the suggestions you've found in this book, you'll start that growth process. Stick with it, even if you find it uncomfortable at first. It will become second nature over time. And you'll find yourself getting the results you've been after all along.

Mastering Business Presentations

Walk into any spotlight knowing that you'll walk out a winner! No matter where or when you're giving a presentation, you'll be cool, clear and persuasive with tactics that make your points come alive, distill your best message and mellow the toughest audience. Use the methods perfected by legendary speakers such as FDR and Abraham Lincoln and by high-profilers Steve Jobs and Jerry Seinfeld. Then enjoy the applause!

$39.95 68 pages

The Truth About Leadership

Reveal your hidden leadership abilities and spur your team to victory. Learn that elusive ability to unite individuals and propel your organization beyond all expectations. Boost your leadership abilities by discovering how to lead through a crisis, the best ways to take on a titan, the right time to burn bridges and much more!

$39.95 65 pages

The Manager's Handbook: 104 Solutions to Your Everyday Workplace Problems

The biggest challenge for managers? Managing your own workload. At last, there's one resource that helps you do everything better. *The Manager's Handbook: 104 Solutions to Your Everyday Workplace Problems* will help you manage better from day one. No lofty theories or buzzwords—just practical advice that helps you get the job done while staying out of legal trouble. This generous handbook is nearly 200 pages long—198, to be exact. Plus it has a generous table of contents to make it easy to find exactly what you need. Solve problems, hire, fire, coach and review employees with confidence.

$59.95 198 pages

$39.95 36 pages

Mastering Business Etiquette & Protocol

This invaluable report reveals the critical connection between protocol and profit, something most people forget, neglect or just never get around to learning in the first place. Discover the how-to of it all, including making proper introductions, writing effective letters, winning back disgruntled customers, handling meetings and special events properly, and much more!

$39.95 40 pages

Mastering Business Finance

Learn how to crunch the numbers like a Wall Street pro! If you want security and job advancement, you need to understand the numbers that drive your company. Use this guide to strip away the intimidation surrounding a complex subject.

$39.95 92 pages

Mastering Business Negotiation

This step-by-step guide is for anyone (even the pushy, impulsive or tongue-tied) who wants a better deal at work, at home and in life! You'll get pointers to build skills in four critical areas and learn to negotiate with forcefulness and grace.

$39.95 84 pages

Mastering Office Politics

How often have you heard that the only way to win at office politics is with dirty tricks? It's really about subtlety, finesse and the artful orchestration of your agenda. This special report contains six sections: advancement, roadblocks, teamwork, leadership, change and managing difficult employees ... each is an instant how-to guide for almost any conceivable political situation.

$39.95 116 pages

Management Resources for Success

Business Management Daily has compiled this collection of resources to help you handle some of the most challenging situations you may face in the workplace.

From dealing with office politics and difficult people to giving performance appraisals that are legal and motivating, we have the do's and don'ts!

Manager's Guide to Effective, Legal Performance Reviews

Make your performance appraisals work for you, not against you! How you conduct an employee's performance review can have a major impact on how that employee behaves. Many books offer general suggestions for improving performance, but few discuss specific ways to make reviews more effective. *Effective, Legal Performance Reviews* shows you how to conduct appraisals with clearly established expectations and no misinterpretation.

$39.95 90 pages

Difficult People at Work

Working with underhanded, self-centered troublemakers is infuriating. This special report will teach you to identify and manage the 24 most challenging personality types and give you proven strategies to put problem people in their place.

$39.95 42 pages

Control the Chaos

Discover field-proven techniques that make it possible for you to leave work every day with a feeling of accomplishment, and improve your reputation with upper management, despite working fewer hours!